Also by Donna Goddard

Fiction
Waldmeer (Book 1 of Waldmeer)
Together (Book 2 of Waldmeer)
Circles of Separation (Book 3 of Waldmeer)
Faith (Book 4 of Waldmeer)
Waldmeer Series: Combined Volume (Books 1 to 4)
Pittown (Book 5 of Waldmeer)
Prana (Book 6 of Waldmeer)

Nonfiction
The Love of Being Loving (Book 1 of Love and Devotion)
The Love of Devotion (Book 2 of Love and Devotion)
Love's Longing
Love, Devotion, and Longing (Combined Volume of The Love of Being Loving, The Love of Devotion, Love's Longing)
Strange Words – A Little Book of Poems and Prayers
Dance: A Spiritual Affair

Cover design by Donna Goddard

Artwork: Catherine of Siena by Toni Carmine Salerno

The Love of Being

Loving

Love and Devotion Series
(Book 1)

Donna Goddard

Contents

Part 2: Healing and Devotion

Introduction

The Love of Being Loving is about awakening and expanding our spiritual consciousness. It is also a personal journey. However, that which is elevating for a single consciousness is also elevating for human consciousness as a whole. There are no secrets. Nothing is withheld by God. Yet, it is only by our own sincere searching, the evolutionary stage we have reached, and the grace of God that we come into contact with spiritual pathways and teachers that are right for us at any particular time. This book is based on the metaphysical teachings of two spiritual paths and their corresponding founders: Dr Thomas Hora of Metapsychiatry and Mary Baker Eddy of Christian Science. The ideas expressed have a universal quality. Spiritual principles, if true, are true for everyone. That is the yardstick that validates their authenticity. Authentic spiritual ideas also have the universal power to heal. Healing is the building block of both individual and collective spiritual evolution.

This edition of *The Love of Being Loving* has many quotes from Thomas Hora and Mary Baker Eddy and also a few other relevant teachers. The quotes lived with me for the years that I studied both spiritual disciplines and were foundational to my learning. They are at the end of each chapter.

Love and Devotion Series

Love and Devotion is a two-book nonfiction series.

The first book, in the series, is *The Love of Being Loving.* It is about the earlier adult years of my spiritual development. Dr Thomas Hora (Metapsychiatry) and Mary Baker Eddy (Christian Science) were the most significant influences on my spiritual path during my twenties and thirties.

The second book is *The Love of Devotion.* In my forties, I started reading a series of metaphysical books by Dr David R. Hawkins. I realised that they were having a potent impact on my growth and Dr Hawkins became my next spiritual teacher. Dr Hawkins (Devotional Nonduality) and Dr Hora came from very similar spiritual and intellectual terrain. We are drawn to a certain field of truth which resonates with our inner leanings. My interest in understanding thought drew me to teachers who also had a deep interest in human consciousness.

Quotes

*Spiritual love, derived from Love-Intelligence, is nonconditional, nonpersonal benevolence. It is **the love of being loving**, with no strings attached, just for the sake of being what God wants us to be. Thomas Hora*

The true theory of the universe, including man, is not in material history but in spiritual development. Mary Baker Eddy

Goodness never fails to receive its reward, for goodness makes life a blessing. As an active portion of one stupendous whole, goodness identifies man with universal good. I am able to impart truth, health, and happiness, and this is my reason for existing. Mary Baker Eddy

Part 1

Love and Intelligence

xiv

Solutions are Spiritual

The Dark Night of the Soul

It is often in the utter despair of humanness that we become willing to consider deeply spiritual answers. It was through the pathway of Metapsychiatry and the guidance and support of its founder, Dr Thomas Hora, that I was able to discover a higher spiritual truth. The door and the guide will be different for most people but once the door is open, we are all in the same territory. Spiritual truth irretrievably alters our way of seeing reality and our ability to heal both ourselves and other people. Most spiritual awakening is due to a total disappointment in the human condition to provide any sense of substantial happiness. It is a blessing in disguise. Our greatest need is for the love and assurance that spiritual understanding brings. If it were not for the common experience of human lovelessness and limitation then we would not be driven to seek a higher love.

My initial contact with Metapsychiatry was through a book that was given to me. Not long after reading the book, I was able to travel to the United States to attend the annual conference of Metapsychiatry. I went with my husband who was an investment banker and twenty years my senior. I was twenty-two at the time and Dr Hora was seventy. His presence radiated peace, assurance, love, and power. He was, in fact, the only person I had ever met who had the quality of being that I was looking for. He instantly became my teacher, without reservation, and with deep longing for growth and spiritual progress.

Some days, back in Australia, I would simply repeat many times, *God loves me. That is enough.* I read the books daily, listened to the class tapes that were sent to me, and prayed all the time. I spoke frequently with Dr Hora on the phone; both from Australia and, for several years, from England (often, in the middle of the night because of the time difference). I was also able to travel to the States, fairly regularly, to see Dr Hora and attend his classes and the annual conferences. All of this occurred before the day of the internet and so international communication was certainly not an easy process.

Once, Dr Hora told me that it was *the dark night of the soul.* He assured me that it would lift and I would be surprised at how happy I would be. Everything he told me, I soaked in desperately. This period was the crucible which was to be of vital and foundational importance in the development of my spiritual understanding.

In all the conversations I had with Dr Hora, the most often repeated and most important concept was,

> *Donna, you have to understand that you are not here to get love. You are here to manifest non-conditional goodness, for God's sake. You are here for God and if you are devoted to that idea you will not be disturbed by what other people believe. You will never feel unloved if you know that that's not what you are here for. We are all here for God and we are to manifest non-personal, nonconditional benevolence, with no strings attached. Love is its own reward. You don't have to worry about what you are getting or not getting. You are here for God. That's the bottom line. Once you learn to live that way, you will never be vulnerable to other people.*

To understand this is to understand *the love of being loving.* It radically changes us. People, in and of themselves, cannot give us happiness. Activities, in and of themselves, cannot give us happiness. At a certain stage of development, one releases all the attachments to both people and activities as a source of happiness. In so doing, one finds a more subtle way of being present in the world. One becomes a loving presence, a centre for Divine grace. Once again, people and activities are enjoyed. In fact, much more so. However, there is no craving or desire to get something, no expectation that the person or activity can fulfil us. One brings something – the love of God.

During this whole period of suffering and mental and spiritual struggling, Dr Hora let me both suffer and struggle. He, at no point, tried to alleviate my suffering by human means – by sympathy, affection or human advice. He knew that if I just kept going, the understanding of nonpersonal, divine Love would come. Happily, it did. The darkness grew less and the light came filtering in to remain a growing presence.

Quotes

Problems are basically psychological, which means interpersonal. Solutions are spiritual, which means omniactional. Thomas Hora

Would existence without personal friends be to you a blank? Then the time will come when you will be solitary, left without sympathy; but this seeming vacuum is already filled with divine Love. When this hour of development comes, even if you cling to a sense of personal joys, spiritual Love will force you to accept what best promotes your growth. Universal Love is the divine way. Mary Baker Eddy

The wintry blasts of earth may uproot the flowers of affection, and scatter them to the winds; but this severance of fleshly ties serves to unite thought more closely to God, for Love supports the struggling heart until it ceases to sigh over the world and begins to unfold its wings for heaven. Mary Baker Eddy

The trend of human life was too eventful to leave me undisturbed in the illusion that this so-called life could be a real and abiding rest. The world was dark. Thus it was when the moment arrived of the heart's bridal to more spiritual existence. When the door opened, I was waiting and watching. Soulless famine had fled. Mary Baker Eddy

The footsteps of thought, rising above material stand-points, are slow, and portend a long night to the traveller; but the angels of His presence – the spiritual intuitions that tell us when 'the night is far spent, the day is at hand' – are our guardians in the gloom. Mary Baker Eddy

Enlightened man loves the loving quality of consciousness, and this enables him to transcend conditions. This is called nonconditional love. For instance, we have to be able to love people who hate us, or who are provocative towards us, or people who envy us, or are jealous, or people who compete with us, or who do not respect us or accept us. The secret to this kind of love is compassion. Thomas Hora

God is our refuge and strength, a very present help in trouble. The Bible

Only God's thoughts constitute my true being. Thomas Hora

There is nothing as important when making ready for the day, as an early morning period of stillness, wherein to make sure that the Truth, and the Truth only, controls our consciousness. However, that the consciousness may be clear enough to perceive the Truth, we must let go of thoughts and sensations of the material world, must be still and know that all that truly exists is Good, and determine to know nothing else. We must also be humble, willing to be taught, to receive, and then when joy has been let into the heart, and gratitude is felt, we are in a condition to receive the blessing – to know the Truth, and we can be assured that Love will guide us, that success will ultimately crown every endeavour, for all things work together for good. Nora Holm

The Two Intelligent Questions

1. What is the meaning of what seems to be?
2. What is what really is? Thomas Hora

The message of Dr Hora was first and foremost that problems have meanings. What are our problems telling us? Physical symptoms and other problems have corresponding thoughts. If we are able to understand these corresponding thoughts, we will have uncovered the meaning of our problems. All problems – physical, mental, emotional, experiential – are reduced to the thoughts which essentially make up the problem. Far from being a handicap, our problems are our guideposts. They point out the many ways in which our thoughts are founded on unhelpful, incorrect, and harmful concepts. Once the meaning of our problems is understood, we can spiritually correct our thinking. This change in thought will inevitably bring some sort of healing. Healing will manifest in a more beautiful, calm, healthy, loving, and beneficial life.

Fundamentally, thought is energy. It is the energy which creates our human experiences. Some ideas prove to be helpful in our lives such as love, happiness, peace, and intelligence. They help us to prosper. Some ideas prove to be troublesome in our lives such as selfishness, fear, jealousy, and anger. They cause us to suffer. In understanding the meaning of our problems, it helps to be aware of *what we cherish, what we hate, and what we fear*. These three factors will be magnets for all sorts of experiences. If we cherish spiritual good then the level of conscious contact with divine Love will be high. Recognising what is cherished, hated, and feared will help us to clarify the underlying thought patterns of any illness or problem.

At the human level, there are problems. These problems have meanings. Understanding the meaning of our problems helps us to spiritually progress. Meanings are the mental equivalent of a problem. They are the thoughts we hold in consciousness which are responsible for our human experiences. How do we uncover a meaning? It takes spiritual intuition, a mature understanding of human nature, honesty about what we are really thinking and feeling, and a willingness to be embarrassed. One of the greatest difficulties for mankind is the inbuilt desire to protect the ego by any means possible. In order to heal, one must first be willing to let go of the desire to protect the ego by instinctive and, often, relentless denial. Spiritual healing requires honesty, humility, lack of pretension, and the ability to receive inspired direction from Mind. Eventually, we come to see life from a higher level, from the divine perspective of *what really is*. This is what our spiritual journey is all about. To understand *what really is* requires a sincere desire to see the good of God at all times, in all of life.

Who Am I Angry At?

One of the main problems that Dr Hora helped me to understand and heal was migraine headaches. The headaches were my barometer. They told me when something was wrong with my mental and spiritual equilibrium which, at the beginning, was all the time. The headaches alerted me to the areas in my life which needed healing. Dr Hora suggested that I ask myself a question whenever I had a headache. The question was to help me understand the meaning of my experience of physical pain. It was, *Who am I angry at?* At first, I could not think of anyone. That was, however, simply because I was not yet aware enough of my thoughts to know that I was angry with a number of people and very angry with a few people in particular.

When I became more aware and realised the extent of my anger, I went on to consider my anger was perfectly justified, as most people who are angry will tell you. One of the most important lessons we learn on the spiritual path is that we cannot be angry with anyone without hurting ourselves. What a hard lesson that is for most of us. We are so very reluctant to give up our blaming, our righteous indignation, our hurt and anger. However, when we realise that our suffering is in direct proportion to our anger, we may have the wisdom and good sense to let it go so that it is not within our conscious or unconscious thoughts anymore. The headaches were gradually healed until even the memory of them held no more fear or reality.

Blame

A positive side effect of working on the meaning of our problems is that we are forced to give up blaming. Nothing could be more beneficial to our spiritual progress. We refrain from blaming our bodies, hereditary factors, economic conditions, our partner, our parents, our upbringing, our boss or any other person. Knowing that our problems have meanings does not mean that we now blame ourselves for our miserable condition instead of other people. It means we understand that our problems are telling us something is not spiritually correct in our thinking. Without reproach or guilt, we understand that we just don't understand enough yet. However, we are going to. That is why we are students on the spiritual path.

We give up self-pity and complaining that life has given us a raw deal and that we are incapable of doing anything about it. Or if we are nice, we won't complain. We will still think that life has given us a raw deal but we won't say it. We will just carry on and be a martyr. Dr Hora frequently said, "To be nice is not so nice." To be a martyr is not spiritually desirable. God

8

does not want martyrs. God wants happy, contributing, healthy, loving souls to demonstrate every strong and beautiful idea of divine Truth.

We take a deep, metaphorical breath, take responsibility for our own well-being, and we study, listen, ponder, confront, and pray until the meanings of our problems are clear. Once meanings are clear, we are then free to accept the spiritual solutions. If we try to skip straight to spiritual solutions, without genuinely understanding the meaning of a problem, we will often find that the problem won't heal. Or if it appears to heal, there is the tendency for it to come back, maybe, in a different form because the thought that is bringing it about is still right there with us.

Telling the Truth

It seems such a simple thing to be authentic, to tell the truth, to be honest. Yet, most of us go to great lengths to avoid it. We do not trust ourselves. Nor do we trust the humanity and compassion of other people. The first great hurdle to spiritual progress is denial. Denial is refusing to tell the truth. When we pass this hurdle and begin to face ourselves honestly, we make large steps forward. In order to become honest, it is usually necessary for us to tame our overactive conscience or as Freud called it, the superego. We have to quieten the superego's parental, judgemental tendencies. We forgive ourselves with the understanding that being human automatically means we have to contend with the naturally selfish and survival-seeking nature of the ego or small self. Our task is to patiently tame the ego into submission so that the loving, divine soul of our being shines forth. If our superego or conscience is too brutal with our failings, we will be forced to protect ourselves and we will not have the courage to face our failings. We progressively learn to tell the

9

truth, forgive ourselves, and turn to the Light in order to grow
more beautiful

Quotes

The physical is mental. Thomas Hora

We ask God to help us to see that the perfection of his creation is already an established fact, that we are joint participants in the good of God. Our work is nothing else than a constant endeavour to improve and increase this realization. The more clearly we can see this, the more our lives will correspond to what really is. Thomas Hora

Anger is an epiphenomenon of frustration. The meaning of anger can be found mainly in one single phrase – 'I want'. Another source of anger is the habit of "should" thinking, namely, thinking in terms of what should be and what should not be. Habits of thoughts and words are our tormentors. Thomas Hora

Nothing can yoke or burden one but one's own thoughts – thoughts of hate, of fear, of lust, of greed, of evil in any form. It is better, however, to liken evil thoughts to veils which hide from one's eyes the Truth, the beauty of things which grow in the sunshine of Love. These veils are thick and of ugly colour. They distort. Many there are who grope about all their lives because they wear such a number; they run into danger, injure themselves and others and finally in seeming darkness they lose their way. The truth is that they were all the time in the light, but they knew it not, for they would wear the veils. God acts upon the assumption that everyone sees clearly, and who would suspect His ever present help when behind so many thicknesses of evil? Nora Holm

11

Much of your pain is self-chosen.
It is the bitter potion by which the physician within
you heals your sick self. Kahlil Gibran

Everything depends upon the thoughts we entertain.
Thomas Hora

Spiritual healing is an aspect of the non-dimensional
realm of reality. It is the perspective of life that is
healed, not material parts of the body. Thomas Hora

What we cherish, what we hate and what we fear, are
highly charged thoughts carrying a powerful energy
level in the direction of manifesting themselves in
visible form. Thomas Hora

Thought is fundamental to life. Essentially, thought is
energy which has the tendency to transmute itself into
phenomena. Invalid thoughts will transmute
themselves into invalid phenomena, which means that
invalid thoughts are harmful, while valid thoughts are
health promoting. It is not a mystery that it is not a
desirable condition of mind to entertain unloving
thoughts. As we grow in the understanding of this
basic principle of transmutation of thought energy,
we will become very careful about what we are
thinking. We may develop a discipline of mind where
we do not indulge ourselves anymore in negative and
existentially invalid thought processes. Thomas Hora

The meaning and purpose of life is to come to know
reality. Thomas Hora

The Eleven Principles of Metapsychiatry

The Principles of Metapsychiatry

1. Thou shalt have no other interests before the good of God, which is spiritual blessedness.

The vast majority of people live their life with innumerable interests before spiritual good and that accounts for the unhappiness that the vast majority of people feel at their most honest soul level. Good relationships, material abundance, fulfilling work, enjoyable and enthralling interests, and glowing health are not excluded by having our undivided attention on the spiritual path. They are an accompaniment to it. For the sincere seeker, qualities such as peace, assurance, gratitude, love, and spiritual good are always of primary and supreme importance.

2. Take no thought for what should be or what should not be; seek ye first to know the good of God, which already is.

Dr Hora would often tell his students that in order to have a more peaceful and harmonious life, we need to lose the *shoulds and should-nots* from our vocabulary. Many arguments, hurt feelings, and personal stalemates would quickly be resolved by the realisation of this principle. Tightly held ultimatums, self-righteous demands, personal tyrannies, and uncompromising interpersonal rules are the fuel of family dysfunction. Freedom and respect go a long way to dissolving family tensions. They help us to release our own interpersonal expectations and they protect us from the stated and silent demands of others. Families frequently have strongly held shoulds and should-nots about many issues. Do we not see the

13

bitter result of this repeatedly? Neither be tyrannised nor tyrannise anyone else.

When spiritual light is turned to the picture of family life, we see things differently. The sweetest families are those where everyone is free to come and go; where everyone is allowed and encouraged to explore their purpose, their best desires, and their individual expression in the world. Much damage is done in ordinary families in the name of loyalty, which is mostly guilt, and under the guise of love, when nothing could be further from the truth. Emotional and spiritual maturity means that we have outgrown our family of birth and its invisible should conditions. We still love our birth families. In fact, we will be better at loving them. However, we will have outgrown the unconscious desire for the love and approval from, generally, less than enlightened family members which always puts us in a vulnerable and detrimental position.

If we take no thought for what should be and what should not be, it does not mean that we will become lazy, selfish, undisciplined, and chaotic. Rather, we will have an overriding sense of the Divine structure and order. Excellence and good character will be driven by the love of goodness and progress, not by fear. Our freedom and peace of mind will be assured. Far from being forgotten or overlooked, we will be loved for our growing graciousness.

3. There is no interaction anywhere, there is only omniaction everywhere.

Dr Hora defined interaction as *thinking about what others are thinking about what we are thinking.* Interaction is the basis of ordinary human life and it is the prime meaning of illness and other problems. Problems are predominantly interactional. From the Divine perspective, there is only omniaction. To discover this is our spiritual life mission. It gives us our freedom from the human dream. It does not mean that we become a recluse. We increasingly become a transparency for universal Love, blessing whoever comes into our range of influence without the negative side-effects of interactional thinking.

4. Yes is good, but no is also good.

It is human nature to want what we want, how and when we want it. However, as we progress, we learn that insisting on what we want is a great source of frustration and distraction. The remedy is as simple and as difficult as saying, *I may not know what is best for me or someone else or the greater plan.* We relax into the flow of life, trusting the Divine heart.

5. God helps those who let him.

To let God help us requires humility and the learned assurance that God is our best bet. This principle can be used consciously whenever choices and decisions confront us. To let God help us means to suspend all calculative thinking, anxiety, worry, and mental agonising about what should be and what should not be. We need the courage which dares to not know in order to discern what the all-knowing knows.

6. If you know what, you know how.

The sixth principle is a reminder to steer clear of operational thinking. If we know that we are deeply and completely loved by Life then we will know how to let it flow through us freely. If we know that the essential force of Life is immensely beautiful and endlessly creative then we will know how to follow our inner guidance. If we know that our true being is spiritually perfect, complete, and pure then we will be healthy, well-balanced, productive, and happy.

7. Nothing comes into experience uninvited.

This principle does not mean that we purposely and consciously invite suffering into our life. Nor does it mean that we are to blame for the, perhaps, less than desirable state of our affairs. It means that the thoughts we entertain in consciousness inevitably draw certain experiences. The first intelligent question, *What is the meaning of what seems to be?* is based on this metaphysical principle. Thoughts translate into experience. Asking the meaning of problems is simply translating experiences back into thoughts. Once our thoughts are understood, we can then alter them, be healed, and grow in our conscious connection with divine Truth.

8. Problems are lessons designed for our edification.

Since nothing comes into experience uninvited, it spontaneously follows that our problems have very specific messages for our spiritual development. Without the pain of problems, very few of us would be interested in giving up our human attachments and ignorance.

9. Reality cannot be experienced or imagined; it can, however, be realized.

Reality cannot be grasped by calculative, imaginative or emotive thinking. It must be discovered by the soul. The soul in us which recognises Reality is part of the greater Soul which is, itself, Reality.

10. The understanding of what really is, abolishes all that seems to be.

This principle forms the basis of spiritual healing.

11. Do not show your pearls to unreceptive minds, for they will demean them.

As we grow in spiritual wisdom, we become naturally astute in our conversations. We do not provoke other people's anger and ridicule by saying truths that ignorant minds are incapable of understanding, and will possibly react aggressively towards in order to protect their own untruthful life force. We develop an intuitive sense of precisely what to say and when to say it. Wise individuals often say very little but what they say tends to hit the mark. Such remarks can remain in the mind of the recipient for a long time, possibly, a lifetime. Wisdom carries power.

Quotes

God only asks one thing – our complete attention. Thomas Hora

The word "should" is a tyrannical one and implies an endeavour to exercise personal control and influence over others. Thomas Hora

Blessed are the shouldless for their lives shall be effortless, efficient and effective. Thomas Hora

Blessed are the shouldless for their lives will be fussless. Thomas Hora

Behold my mother and my brethren! For whosoever shall do the will of my Father which is in heaven, the same is my brother, and sister, and mother. The Bible

The principle of harmonious living is as follows; take no thought for what should be or what should not be. Seek ye first to know the harmony and joy of soul existence, the good of God. Thomas Hora

When we say that there is no interaction anywhere, we mean that a great deal of suffering comes from expecting love from other people and building our lives on that idea. If we are living in that context or with that mind-set, then we are vulnerable, insecure and easily disturbed. But if we understand love as the essence of God expressing itself through us freely as goodness, intelligence, generosity and assurance, then love is a spiritual sea, a medium in which we 'live and move and have our being' [Acts 17:28]. No one can deprive us of the happiness and assurance of knowing that we are living expressions of divine love. Thomas Hora

When we are habitually involved in contemplating our relationships with other people there is static in consciousness. This interferes with inspiration, with creativity, with healing, with peace, assurance, gratitude, and love. Thomas Hora

Enlightened man neither seeks interaction nor shuns it. To him it is just a dream of life as a person. Thomas Hora

Conscious union with God doesn't exclude people. It makes harmonious co-existence possible. Thomas Hora

Unenlightened life is characterized by a great deal of intentionality. We want and we don't want. A beholder doesn't intend anything. He is just glowing with the constant awareness of Love-Intelligence, filling the universe with its omnipresence. Thomas Hora

In proportion that we understand our inseparability from the good of God, from God's presence, we will be able to let go of the compulsion to be in control. Thomas Hora

To many, this may seem like foolish passivity, or even irresponsible "do nothingness." But, in fact, this is neither negligence, nor apathy, nor passiveness, nor aggressiveness. It is alert reverent responsiveness which forms the basis of enlightened, creative and intelligent decisiveness. Thomas Hora

Nothing comes into experience uninvited. Thoughts entertained in consciousness express themselves either in words or actions, and they have a tendency to attract corresponding experiences. Therefore, this can also be called the law of correspondence. Thomas Hora

Existence apart from God is an illusion. The right understanding of our selfhood is based on the realization of our inseparability from the divine Mind, the creative Principle of the universe. Through this realization we discover our true self-identity in the context of God. Thomas Hora

We are not afraid of problems. We welcome them; we face them and use them as counterpoints for the realization of truth. Thus, not only are we healed of problems, but we also make a step forward on the way to enlightenment. Thomas Hora

Love can only be realized. What does it mean to realize something? It means to become conscious of the reality of something. When we realize love, we discover that love really is; and that which is, does not have to be produced since it already is. We become aware of it by the quality of our presence. Such presence has a healing, harmonizing, enlightening impact on whatever situation we happen to be participating in. Thomas Hora

We must learn to maintain a constant, conscious awareness of the perfect harmony of divine reality. Thomas Hora

Only the right realization of the one Mind will give us peace and enable us to look at the battleground and see that everything, everywhere, is peaceful. There's a bloody battle going on all the time if we judge by appearances. But when we judge with 'enlightened judgment,' we can discern that everything, everywhere, is peaceful and good and intelligent and harmonious. There is no conflict; there is no strife – there is only one Mind, and this Mind is in control of the whole universe. Right where strife seems to be, there is harmony because the one Mind is in charge, regardless of appearances to the contrary. Thomas Hora

Wisdom is the principal thing; therefore get wisdom and with all thy getting get understanding. The Bible

Relationships and Interaction

While we are learning to recognise spiritual reality, we are also learning to understand the complexities of normal human interaction. We are learning to understand the meaning and purpose of our interactional problems. Interactional problems are our lessons. We are trying to draw the specific and individual lessons from our problems which will help our spiritual growth. Relationships are one of the more painful and also delightful of teaching mediums. Our closest relationships will generally have the most opportunity for both pain and progress. Unlike the common misperception that relationships are for the purpose of making us happy, relationships are generally more suited to making us grow.

When we understand the educational significance of our relationships, we will consciously use them for the purpose of spiritual growth. We will no longer run away from the problems we have. We will welcome the opportunity to further develop our own understanding and that of the other person. This takes courage and honesty. It means facing our own thoughts and allowing our less than desirable, unconscious thoughts to come to the surface. It helps to remind ourselves in this, sometimes, painful process that regardless of our frequently ugly and fearful thoughts we are, nevertheless, a loved child of God. In our true and spiritual essence, we are beautiful, good, and pure. The rest is just a mistake. This helps us to face our negative thoughts without condemnation and despair.

The lessons of other people are between them and God. We cannot force, organise, cajole, intimidate, deceive or plead with anyone to do or know anything which they do not sincerely and honestly wish for themselves. Of all people, this applies foremost to our partner and our children. Forgiveness, compassion, and letting-be are spiritually vital qualities. This allows others the space to grow in their own time and in their own way. Although we cannot force the issue of another's development, just being around a spiritually aware individual provides many opportunities for growth. We can daily demonstrate spiritual principles in the context of ongoing life. Our honest spiritual progress will have a beneficial and encouraging impact on those around us. Life will have its own way of dealing with the consistently ignorant thoughts of those who have no desire to learn. In the end, life will tolerate only for so long harmful or self-destructive thoughts and behaviours. The inevitable consequences will fall into place, one way or another.

As well as the honesty that is required by each individual in confronting his or her own issues, we must also acknowledge the shared lessons of the relationship. There needs to be open and meaningful although, generally, uncomfortable discussion. If we have a long-term relationship and we would like it to continue in a healthy way, we have no choice but to clearly discuss those important issues which need healing. If we do not, the relationship will most likely deteriorate into a great mass of unconscious resentments and fears which, in turn, will lead to unhappiness, illness or other serious problems. One way or another, ignorant thoughts will always find an avenue of expression. They will either be honestly seen for what they are or, if such honesty is not permitted, they will come out in another form. Thought, as energy, needs to find an avenue of expression. We can work on and heal detrimental tendencies before they manifest as devastating consequences in our life experience.

The Prayer of Right Seeing

Everyone and everything is here for God whether they know it or not. Thomas Hora

First, we learn to understand the meaning or dynamic of the human interaction which makes up the fabric of the shared human existence. While we are becoming more proficient at this, we are also becoming increasingly able to recognise the omniaction that is everywhere. We see life with different eyes. Everyone and everything is here for God whether they know it or not. The gradual evolution of consciousness is through the ranks of interaction and then into the invisible but mighty domain of spirit. It is a blessed and satisfying path and each step is rewarded with greater health, success, peace, and fulfilment. The struggles in outgrowing mistaken concepts are well worth it and quickly forgotten when one is bathing in the light and freedom of a progressively evolving capacity to live from one's soul.

The Sound of One Hand Clapping

Removing oneself from interactional thinking and behaviour provides an exit from the stresses and pains of the ego's perspective. It opens the door to the possibility of *joint participation in the good of God.* Joint participation in the good of God is the awakening of the divine Presence in a loving and mutually beneficial partnership. During the decade I studied with Dr Hora, another idea which was very helpful to me was *the sound of one hand clapping.* Spiritual students commonly find that even though they may be interested in the divine presence, generally, other people are not. Most people are interested in interaction or clapping. Our job is to lessen the interactional noise and to elevate the mental climate by, mostly, silent acknowledgement of the allness of God's good.

This brings to mind a healing of one of Dr Hora's patients. A man who had been seeing him was suffering from severe back pain. During the session the man had been complaining bitterly about his daughter. Dr Hora thought, *Nevertheless, you love her very much.* He said nothing but silently and

24

peacefully knew the nothingness of interactional problems and the allness of God's supreme, encompassing, pervading Love. Suddenly, the man stopped complaining, stood up, and declared with amazement that the back pain had disappeared. *The sound of one hand clapping* may seem somewhat contradictory to the idea of honest discussion within a relationship. However, we are talking about different levels of consciousness. While we are in the human experience, it is important to think, speak, and act in a way which is most conducive to healing problems and to facilitating the healthful and positive development of our relationships.

At a higher level, our spiritual sense of what is really taking place lifts us into a different dimension where interaction and relationships no longer have the reality and power that they have in the lower human world. However, we must not deceive ourselves about our human frailties and life conditions. Honesty is required at every step, in every way. Our human experience is then naturally lightened as a result of dawning consciousness. At the human level, we need a certain type of wisdom in order to maintain our well-being. When we see life from the higher perspective, human issues lose some of their power and relevance. From this perspective, human progress is not really the point. Progress implies something needing improvement. Spiritual reality does not need improving. A perfect order needs nothing but to be seen. This does not mean that we abandon the human detail and become reckless and uncaring in our affairs. Rather, the human becomes increasingly pervaded with the knowledge of divine principles which clarify, heal, uplift, and transform it.

Quotes

When love beckons to you, follow him,
Though his ways are hard and steep.
For even as love crowns you so shall he crucify you.
Even as he is for your growth so is he for your
pruning. Kahlil Gibran

And think not you can direct the course of love,
for love, if it finds you worthy, directs your course.
Kahlil Gibran

Love one another, but make not a bond of love;
Sing and dance together and be joyous,
but let each one of you be alone. Kahlil Gibran

Give your hearts, but not into each other's keeping.
For only the hand of Life can contain your hearts.
Kahlil Gibran

The Christ within us has infinite compassion,
understanding, and forgiveness. We can remind
ourselves that there seems to be two of us. One is the
human person, which is a fantasy, and the other is the
Christ-consciousness, the potential of infinite Love-
Intelligence and the actuality of it, which can be
realized or unrealized. We are always working to
realize it to the utmost possible extent. Thomas Hora

The sound of one hand clapping is a Zen Buddhist
koan [riddle] which stands for the ability to transcend
the pressures and the temptations which enter into
interaction thinking and behaviour. It is based on a
constant, conscious awareness of the presence and

the power of omniactive Mind, the governing principle of life. Thomas Hora

What if one is married to a partner who is not interested in the good of God? This is a situation where the spiritually minded partner must learn to hear the sound of one hand clapping. Thomas Hora

In transcendence we rise and expand our conscious awareness into the full-dimensional mode of thinking, and the context of our reasoning includes God, Love-Intelligence, the Source of all energy, wisdom, love, power, freedom, and creativity. Once we attain a transcendent perspective on reality, everything changes, just as when we climb up a mountain, the view is entirely different than it was in the valley. As man attains the realization of his full potential, the various concepts which were previously considered very scientific and important, lose their validity, and life is seen entirely differently. For instance, the concepts of interpersonal relationships and marital relationships disappear, and in their place there emerges a discovery of joint participation in the good of God, which makes harmonious coexistence possible. Thomas Hora

The idea of love between persons is an insufficient basis for marriage, but the idea of love as a contextual basis for living with someone is valid. The idea of love between two persons is a narrow-minded way of seeing life, but love can be seen in a broader sense as constituting the spiritual environment in which a marriage can thrive and be securely founded. Thomas Hora

Forgiveness and Compassion

A Holy Process

As spiritual students, forgiveness is fundamental to our spiritual progress and peace of mind. However, when we are hurting, it can feel like a mighty struggle to eliminate the blame. Forgiveness is a holy process and, as such, we receive Divine assistance. We can refuse to allow space within our consciousness for criticism and resentment. We persist in seeing the spiritual identity of ourselves, others, and everything in life. When, eventually, the presence of peace rests in and around us, we can know that we have gained our freedom.

Forgiving is easier when we understand that forgiving someone else means that we are freeing ourselves of an unnecessary burden. Once we are firmly on the path of forgiveness, we will, generally, find that this process spontaneously leads to the lifting of repressions and the healing of memories. This process is a natural and helpful coincidence of being interested in forgiveness. Further, we will find that with every repressed hurt that is lifted and with every painful memory that is being healed, our happiness, lightness, joy, and peace will noticeably increase. Dr Hora often commented that, "Unless we can remember, we will not be able to forget."

The Healing of Memories

When the healing process of forgiveness is underway, previously buried hurts and sadness start to surface. We can cope with their appearance and are ready to do the necessary work on healing them. For example, it is not uncommon for individuals to suddenly start grieving a loss that happened many years ago. Often, this is brought on by the occurrence of another, more recent loss or simply because the student is now capable of healing it. Not only do memories surface in order to be healed but, also, specific people from our past will tend to appear either in person or in our dreams. The purpose of this is to deepen the healing process. It may be that we need to forgive the person or it may be that we need to forgive ourselves for what we did to or thought about that person.

Many spiritual traditions and healing programs stress the importance of this type of healing. Alcoholics Anonymous, for example, has a number of recovery steps which include making a list of all people that the alcoholic felt he or she had harmed and making amends to them, except when to do so would injure them or others. A. A. is an unusually successful self-help group. This success is due to the wonderful, uplifting, and liberating spiritual basis upon which it is founded.

Compassion

On the way to acquiring spontaneous compassion for all beings, there are many times when the basic practice of forgiveness is necessary. We can pray that the soul of the other person and ourselves is joined in the unity of God's all-encompassing love. Being reminded that there is love in every situation, even if it seems absent, helps to dissolve personal anger. Practising the art of forgiveness with individual people is the forerunner to a general compassionate state of consciousness. The consciousness gradually develops the capacity to transmit nonpersonal compassion for all life forms. We pass through the valley of forgiveness, letting go, surrendering anger, and releasing of resentments. This brings us closer to seeing everyone as God's innocent child. As the practice of forgiveness proceeds, there is less need for such a disciplined approach to forgiveness. An advanced state of unforced compassion replaces it. We will not have to fight for every bit of mental freedom. We enter the wonderful realm of compassion. Here the battle subsides. At the point of compassion, the struggle ceases. Compassion is the sweet and effortless consequence of seeing life from a higher perspective.

Faking Forgiveness

Forgiveness and compassion cannot be humanly done, forced or faked. Pretension is always a disability. It excludes the very spiritual qualities we desire. Repressed emotions transmute themselves into physical symptoms. It is unsafe to pretend to be something we are not yet capable of expressing. Pretending a more developed level of consciousness than we are currently capable of holding can inadvertently be responsible for harmful consequences. Physical illness and mental and emotional problems such as depression are, frequently, expressions of repressed emotions. It is better to be ignorant and honest about it than ignorant and dishonest about it. The former leaves the door open for improvement. It also somewhat protects everyone by virtue of the openness of the ignorant thoughts. The latter firmly closes the door on improvement. The combination of ignorance and dishonesty leads to mental manipulation. Such manipulation often results in confusion and despair in the lives of those close to the damaging person.

Recognition, Regret, and Reorientation

Recognition, regret, release, and reorientation are all components of the healing process. *Recognition* is seeing our error and admitting to ourselves and, sometimes, to others that we have made a mistake. We realise that something we said, did or thought was not conducive to what is good. *Regret* is being genuinely sorry. *Release* is letting it go, having compassion for ourselves and knowing that we did the best we could with the way we saw things at the time. *Reorientation* is correcting our thinking, replacing harmful thoughts with better ones, and moving forward to the Light to enjoy a higher quality of Life.

Quotes

The simplest way to define forgiveness is to give up blaming. This means we have to separate the individual from the ignorant ideas which have governed his behaviour. In this manner we are relieved of the pressure of blaming a person. We come to see that the enemy is always ignorance and miseducation. When there is no person to blame, our grievances fizzle out of consciousness, and while we may hate ignorance in any form, it is not possible to carry a grudge against it. Thomas Hora

When there is a sincere desire to forgive, then God gives us the power and the wisdom and the love to accomplish this holy process. Thomas Hora

We need to see ourselves in an entirely different context. We drop the context of the interpersonal, and we see ourselves in the context of God. We are talking about a holy process which is taking place in the context of divine Love-Intelligence. Thomas Hora

This is only possible if we understand that by forgiving people, we are not doing them a favour; we are doing ourselves a favour. We are hurting ourselves by carrying a grudge, and that is no way to live. We must forgive endlessly, continually. We must forgive our parents; we must forgive our siblings, our friends and our enemies. As long as we hate someone and carry a grudge, we are not able to be conscious spiritual beings, because a spiritual being is a manifestation of Love-Intelligence. Thomas Hora

Prayer of Reconciliation

I forgive you and you forgive me.
You and I are one in God.
I am grateful to you and you are grateful to me.
You and I are one in God.
I love you and you love me.
You and I are one in God.
I bless you and you bless me.
You and I are one in God.
Unknown

Does this mean we have to actually say, I forgive you? No, there is nothing to express; this is a battle which takes place in 'the secret place of the most High,' in consciousness. Thomas Hora

A startling thing happens when we become interested in the issue of forgiveness. People who are sincerely interested in the process of forgiveness begin to discover that suddenly they keep remembering long-forgotten hurts. It is almost as if a lid on a pandora's box is opened, and these memories begin to seep through and come into awareness, almost as if they came to be forgiven. As long as there is a desire to blame and punish, these memories remain repressed, but the moment there is a readiness to forgive, then the memories come up. Thomas Hora

Ignorance is inevitable but not necessary. Thomas Hora

But if we start the process of forgiveness, suddenly people who we haven't seen for years may begin to turn up, call us, or ask to see us. They come to be loved, and they come to be forgiven without realizing this. They may come to us in our dreams. This process will heal us and set us free for further growth. Thomas Hora

We seldom suffer from other people. We suffer from what we want and what we don't want. We have to examine conscientiously our secret thoughts about others. Is there something we want or is there something we don't want? This must be dropped. If another individual has certain problems, that is his or her business. If we find those problems painful or troublesome, it may indicate that we want something. We cannot want anything from another. We are not here to get something, but to manifest something. If we learn to be here for God, we are able to view another with compassion and there will be no problems. God is the source of all good, wisdom and love. Compassion frees us from entanglements. Thomas Hora

What is compassion? We define it as understanding the lack of understanding. The compassionate person does not get provoked or impatient. He does not recriminate, judge, condemn, or react personally to other individuals' various misconceptions about life or issues. He is a model of spiritual maturity, a radiancy of Love-Intelligence, clarifying whatever darkness comes before him. He does not demand that another individual get well. He respects an individual's right to be sick or to make no progress at all. Thomas Hora

Compassion is the point where we don't have to forgive anymore. Once we have learned compassion, there will be no need to go through the arduous process of forgiveness. Thomas Hora

We have compassion for ourselves and we say, "Well, I may have these feelings and I may have these thoughts, but I don't have to be involved with them because there is something higher and better for me to pay attention to." Unless we have compassion towards ourselves, how will we ever have compassion for others? We can reach a point where it becomes clear to us that our sick thoughts are no part of our true being. Thomas Hora

Repressed emotions transmute themselves into physical symptoms. Thomas Hora

Many well-meaning religious people, having been educated in the desirability of compassion and nonjudgmentalism – 'Judge not that ye be not judged not' – try not to be condemnatory. This is a difficult task. One tries to behave in a compassionate way. This however does not work. What happens is that we repress our emotional reactions in order to hold up certain images of Christian conduct. Repressed emotions transmute themselves into physical symptoms. It is dangerous to pretend to be compassionate if we are not – even if we mean well – because we haven't as yet reached that level of spiritual maturity. Thomas Hora

There is only one beneficial attitude or quality of mind, and that is compassion. We neither condone nor condemn ignorance. We do not blame or castigate ourselves for not being fully enlightened yet, or for catching ourselves with unloving thoughts. We just recognize, regret, release and reorient ourselves with compassion. Compassion makes healing possible because condemnation, disapproval, arguing, pressuring and trying to change people – including ourselves – is counterproductive. Thomas Hora

Beneficial Presence in the World

The Four W's

1. Who am I? I am an image and likeness of God, a manifestation of Love-Intelligence.
2. What am I? I am a divine consciousness.
3. Where am I? I live and move and have my being in omniactive divine Mind.
4. What is my purpose? My purpose is to be a beneficial presence in the world. (Thomas Hora)

In order to become a beneficial presence in the world, we must have established a strong sense of Divine solitariness within ourselves. Being popular or not, having company or being alone are not issues of concern for the developed soul. A beneficial presence knows that he or she has a job to do and fulfilling that mission is their focus, happiness, and passion. A beneficial presence is a responder not a *do-er.* Our churches, charities, helping professions, education facilities, and many well-functioning families are constituted of people striving to do the right thing, to be a help, and to make some positive contribution to life. However, when we are on the spiritual path, we learn that there is a superior way which does not do harm as well as good. It does not make us tired, run-down, and burnt-out. It blesses everyone, including ourselves. It is the way of the beneficial presence – inspired, perfectly timed, and just right for the situation. It is that which tells a healer what to see, a friend what to say, a parent what to know, a loved one when to hold on and when to let go, a mentor when to comfort and when to confront, and a spiritual student when to go within and when to walk the marketplace.

Prayer and Meditation

Prayer and meditation connect us with who we really are. It does not matter in which way we do this, so long as we do connect with divine Reality and we do it as often as we can until our connection is permanent and unbroken. The purpose of prayer and meditation is not to get something for ourselves but to be here for God which, in turn, will give us more than we need. They are the basis upon which we become a beneficial presence in the world. We then have the capacity to hold all things in the context of the infinite Omnipresence. They sustain our spiritual consciousness. They are a moment-by-moment renewal of our connection with the divine source.

Unsolicited Solicitude

Unsolicited solicitude is unrequested help which is, frequently, no help at all. We do not always have to be asked for help with words. Often, the deepest and most sincere pleas for assistance are communicated nonverbally. However, we must be completely honest with ourselves in recognising what is a sincere request for help and what is not. If unsure, we can make a move – a comment, thought or prayer – in the right direction. If it is consciously or unconsciously blocked by such responses as arguing, disinterest, feigned interest, apathy, belligerence or anger we can assume that our help is not really being requested. In this case, we will simply practice the art of letting be until, and if, such time as there is a genuine interest in our offer of assistance.

The Four Horsemen

Dr Hora spoke about the galloping evils of the *Four Horsemen* as being envy, jealousy, rivalry, and malice. They are quick, escalating, powerful, and a real danger for the unaware. The driving force of hatred will, most likely, be one of these horsemen. We do not have to invite them. They are an inevitable part of human interaction, and all the more so if we are successful in some area. Although we cannot stop them, we can wisely sidestep them. Knowledge is safety.

Those who are not psychologically sophisticated, do not realise the extent to which the average person is unconsciously motivated by jealousy and envy. People who are not happy, confident, and fulfilled will generally resent those who are happier, more confident, and more fulfilled than them. Admiration and envy seem to be received in equal proportion as one develops and succeeds. Many famous people are admired with a passion and also hated with a vengeance. Powerful political leaders are respected and also ruthlessly criticised. Famous movie stars are followed with relentless and undying interest in all details of their life. They are adored and also grossly invaded and scrutinised.

The human world is full of envy, jealousy, rivalry, and malice. When we first learn to recognise these human foibles, we may become somewhat overwhelmed by them and feel that an isolated life would be rather nice. With progress, our focus changes and we learn to think *not what the world is doing to us but what we are doing for the world*. Our attention is not on how the world is hurting us but on how our presence is helping to heal the world. This outward and upward focus is our protection and our guide. At a higher level, we become increasingly aware that the human dream, the human drama (with all its questionable, damaging, and often malevolent intention), is not real life at all. What a marvellous relief that is, given the apparent paltry state of human consciousness. We learn to see an entirely different reality.

Types of Spiritual Students

1. The knower who wants to be known as knowing.
2. The thinker who wants to hone his personal mind.
3. The thief who gathers information in order to possess it.
4. The dreamer who is pleasure-oriented.
5. The hitch-hiker who only "goes along for the ride."
6. The sincere seeker after the truth who seeks redemption and attainment of the faculty of compassion.
7. The finder. (Thomas Hora)

There are a range of spiritual students: the knower, the thinker, the thief, the dreamer, the hitch-hiker, the sincere seeker, and the finder. Only the sincere seeker will make significant progress and become the finder. The knower acquires new knowledge and displays his already accumulated knowledge. The thinker tries to master his personal mind. The thief steals whatever is worth taking in order to use it for a perceived gain. The dreamer fantasises about all the ways in which he is going to improve his life without ever facing the hard facts or doing the individual spiritual work. The hitch-hiker goes along for the ride out of curiosity and desire for entertainment. On the other hand, the sincere seeker is present and awake with bright eyes, searching questions, honest self-confrontation, humility, respect, and gratitude. Success is assured. How do we become a sincere seeker? Dr Hora would say, "We become sincere by being sincere." It is radical, pure intention. How do we become the finder? By the grace of God.

The Door to Joy

One of Dr Hora's most frequent sayings was, "Gratitude is the door to joy." Life is often unfair, disappointing, unloving, and hurtful. It can be difficult to rise to a happy state of being. Gratitude can help us move to a better level of consciousness. To be grateful means to be conscious that life has a divine origin and that it is good. Our problems will then have a tendency to lessen and often disappear. Healing can spontaneously occur when we move from one level of consciousness to a higher one. We automatically align with higher truths which are innately more life enhancing. Under such conditions the individual is self-correcting and self-healing at all levels of their being – physical, emotional, mental, and spiritual.

When we maintain a conscious connection with gratitude, our presence will naturally radiate a certain beauty and undisturbed, inner tranquillity. Such individuals glow. It is the glow which is channelled and expressed by those who are connected with the grand and omnipresent light of Divinity. All such individuals look beautiful and seem irresistible to those who value goodness. They have an attractor field of loveliness which likewise tends to bring out the beauty in other people. All of creation tends to respond positively and lovingly to such a presence.

Quotes

A beneficial presence is a representative of God's qualities. Thomas Hora

A solitary individual is a beneficial presence in the world, and he is neither involved nor uninvolved with other individuals. He is not moving towards people or against people or away from people. He is standing as an individual manifestation of God's presence in the world. Thomas Hora

A solitary individual is not caught up in dualistic anxiety about being in or being out, being liked and accepted or not – all this is nonsense to him. It doesn't disturb him. He never thinks in those terms. He has a glorious sense of freedom. Thomas Hora

He is always a beneficial presence in the world, whether people like him or don't like him, approve of him or disapprove of him. He beholds himself as a certain presence around which all things work together for good. He becomes a focal point of harmony, peace and healing, in the midst of turmoil. Thomas Hora

Being has nothing to do with passivity or activity. A beneficial presence is in no way passive, but neither is he aggressive. He is harmoniously, intelligently, creatively responsive to the demands of life. Thomas Hora

A beneficent person has an operational approach to life. He is someone who thinks that there is something to be done and proceeds to do it according to his own calculative judgments, preconceptions, and decisions. A beneficial presence is a responder. He responds to manifest needs upon promptings from divine Intelligence. One is a human activity, the other is a divinely inspired response. The first is always artificial and is good and bad. The other is always creative, loving, intelligent – and always appropriate. Thomas Hora

What is meditation? Meditation is a wholehearted attentiveness to what God wants. What is the right motivation for meditation? The right motivation for meditation is a sincere interest in committing oneself to being here for God. Thomas Hora

We see that we are emanations of divine Mind and so is everyone else, and when this is clearly established in consciousness, we are beholding ourselves and others – in general and in particular – in the context of divine Reality which is infinite, timeless, spaceless, and completely perfect. Thomas Hora

Prayer and meditation are like spiritual breathing. Thomas Hora

We reach a point of complete quietude, where there are no more thoughts, and we do not have to think about the one Mind – there is only a state of awareness which the Buddhists call 'emptiness'. In this emptiness, God rushes in with a message or an idea, and we can then hear the soundless voice of God, speaking to whatever need happens to be before us at the time when we are meditating. We can be healed – whatever has bothered us will be healed in that emptiness. Thomas Hora

Man has no right to influence anyone; it is however, his duty to God to be influential. How are we to understand that? We become influential by embodying the right values and by making valid statements about what is intelligent, what is good, what is helpful, what is creative, what is beautiful, what is wholesome and leaving it up to others to accept it or reject it. Thomas Hora

Unsolicited solicitude is tyranny and trespassing. Thomas Hora

Love is letting-be. Letting be is reverence for life. Thomas Hora

Letting be is regard for an individual's right to proceed at a speed which God determines for his growth. Thomas Hora

We can transcend the ignorant attitudes and expressions of the world. We are aware of provocation, intimidation, hatred, anger, jealousy, rivalry and malice, but we are not reacting to these ignorant attitudes. We transcend them. We have compassion for the individual and we can forgive him because we have outgrown the habit of blaming. Thomas Hora

The process of spiritual maturation entails, among other things, the outgrowing of the galloping evils of the four horsemen. The four horsemen are: envy, jealousy, rivalry and malice. Envy is a desire to have what someone else has. Jealousy is a desire to be what someone else is. Rivalry is a desire to be better than someone else. Malice is ill will. Thomas Hora

A world of evil, destruction, malice, envy and despair. All this we must learn to forgive, not because we are being "good" and "charitable", but because what we are seeing is not true. A Course in Miracles

The Prayer of Glowing

Now the Eye of my eyes is open
Now the Ear of my ears hears
Now the Mind of my mind knows
Now the Love of my love glows.
Thomas Hora

Gratitude is the door to joy. Thomas Hora

Anyone who glows is very beautiful regardless of physical structure. There is an inner quiet joy which comes from awareness of God's good. Thomas Hora

Don't Make a Move Without God

Several years before Dr Hora's passing, I had reached a point where I no longer had the driving need for his constant guidance. All the ideas I had been daily studying for more than ten years, all the mental resolve to see life from a higher perspective, all the work I had invested in understanding the specific meaning of my problems, and all the countless spiritual corrections and promptings Dr Hora had given me over the years had paved the way for a certain amount of spiritual confidence, independence, and mental freedom.

A year or so before his passing, my life changed direction with the ending of my marriage. I did not discuss it with Dr Hora as I felt it was a spiritually solitary matter between God and myself. There was nothing more that my teacher could have said to me that he had not already said. There were several spiritual truths that were foremost in my thoughts at this time. Dr Hora often taught: *Don't make a move without God. Don't do anything until you've learned what you need to learn.* These two statements were a silent guide throughout my marriage. It is not in anyone's best, long-term interest to make precipitous moves until God lets us know that it is time for a change.

The hard-won spiritual victories that I had long sought were starting to radiate a field of positive and nurturing energy around me. I had an improved sense of peace and of being centred and settled. I was beginning to grasp the higher, nonpersonal concept of love. We are here to express God's universal love, not to be enmeshed in the endless struggles of ordinary, precarious human relationships. I was grateful that my life was able to take a liberating step in a new direction. The outward details of my life could now reflect more closely my inward spiritual growth. Our spiritual progress is inevitably accompanied by better human circumstances, in one way or another.

A Rare Encounter

An encounter with a compassionate being is both rare and innately healing. That was certainly the case with Dr Hora. His students found him to be unusually insightful and very compassionate. The combination of truth and love creates a healing frequency.

Just before Dr Hora's passing, he said to some of his students,

> *Be grateful and remember that God is the only Lover and that God is the only Love. If we are grateful in this way then our love is nonpersonal; it is an awareness of God's Good, and this is real freedom. We are grateful for whatever good comes into our experience, what is intelligent and what is liberating. If we are conscious of being grateful, then there are no problems.*

What Really Is

Dr Hora's work with students was, largely, in helping them understand the meaning of their problems. However, he was able to delve into the hazardous world of human meanings and remain spiritually focused, calm, loving, and nonpersonally involved because he understood the answer to the second intelligent question, *What is what really is?* It was his understanding of *what really is* that healed his students of the thoughts that brought about their problems. When I was studying with Dr Hora, my spiritual work was mostly with meanings; understanding them in myself and in other people. I was in the early stages of seeing an emerging spiritual reality. I had moved address to a world which was not yet clearly understood or recognised for its true magnificence and power. As time progressed, spiritual existence was no longer such a newly dawning reality. It was beginning to have the clarity and wonder of a clear, bright morning.

Quotes

If you can see all others as God's children then your love becomes universal rather than personal. Thomas Hora

The more we understand Reality – the truth of being – the more light is reaching our consciousness, and this light abolishes the darkness of our cherished assumptions. Therefore, it is the light of truth which brings about what appears to be a change. Actually, nothing has to change. Only darkness has to be dispelled by the light of truth. Thomas Hora

When the ocean is stirred by a storm, then the clouds lower, the wind shrieks through the tightened shrouds, and the waves lift themselves into mountains. We ask the helmsman: "Do you know your course? Can you steer safely amid the storm?" He answers bravely, but even the dauntless seaman is not sure of his safety. Yet, acting up to his highest understanding, firm at the post of duty, the mariner works on and awaits the issue. Thus should we deport ourselves on the seething ocean of sorrow. Hoping and working, one should stick to the wreck, until an irresistible propulsion precipitates his doom or sunshine gladdens the troubled sea. Mary Baker Eddy

The best way to enlighten others is to be models of spiritual maturity. We are teaching not with our words but with our life. Thomas Hora

An encounter with a compassionate individual has great therapeutic impact. It is a rare experience to meet someone who doesn't judge, who doesn't seek to find fault or condemn. Usually wherever we turn, people are in the habit of judging, criticizing, evaluating, bombarding us with personal questions, and assuming that we are guilty until proven innocent. This is the way of the world, and therefore any encounter in the spirit of true compassion can be – and often is – a healing experience. Thomas Hora

Be grateful and remember that God is the only Lover and that God is the only Love. If we are grateful in this way then our love is nonpersonal; it is an awareness of God's Good, and this is real freedom. We are grateful for whatever good comes into our experience, what is intelligent and what is liberating. If we are conscious of being grateful, then there are no problems. Thomas Hora

We cannot change anyone and we cannot change ourselves. But we can gradually become interested in and turn to the light, and this light abolishes the darkness of a sense of personhood and the calculative mind. Then we see the underlying pre-existent truth of an individual as a divine consciousness of Love-Intelligence emerging. And it appears that a great change has taken place – which we call transformation or healing – but actually nothing has changed. That which was hidden has become visible. Thomas Hora

Part 2

Healing and Devotion

Metaphysics

New Relationship

A few years after Dr Hora's passing, early one morning just before waking, I felt the presence of two beings in my room. One of them was my friend's mother. She had passed on the day before. The other was an angelic being. Its radiance was pure, uncontaminated, loving, and powerful without exerting any effort. It had no heaviness of self-centred thought or even self-awareness such as humans have. Neither said anything but I could tell that the woman was very worried about her son. I heard myself say to the woman, "Don't worry about your son. I will take care of him." The woman was relieved, looked at the angel who indicated that it was time to go, and they both left. Even though her son and I were friends, we were not close friends and he was involved in another relationship. My pledge seemed a rather illogical one. About a year later, we did indeed start a relationship and not long after that he became involved in a lengthy court case with serious consequences to his life. We also had an unexpected pregnancy and the arrival of a child during this period. All of this was naturally very challenging. The course of love and loyalty is a mysterious one but who are we not to follow its instinctive lead?

New Pathway

When I first became a serious student of metaphysics at the age of twenty-two, I studied all the metaphysical writings that I could get my hands on. I was a very dedicated student and an avid reader and so I read a lot of books in this field of study. Dr Hora and some of his students in New York introduced me to Christian Science as one of the metaphysical schools of thought.

Back in Australia, I visited some Christian Science churches but, even then, the churches were empty and seemed to only have senior citizens. I remember being highly offended that one gentleman at the door politely asked me if I wished to go to the Sunday School. I was in my early twenties but I looked young. I did not realise Sunday School in Christian Science went until the age of twenty. I came from a Catholic background where Sunday School was for children. I felt like saying, "What are you talking about? I am married and I am a very serious spiritual student, not a child playing in the Sunday School." I continued my metaphysical studies at home, loving all my treasured spiritual books.

Once my little children started attending a Christian Science-based school, Christian Science naturally became a significant part of our lives, not just a private part of my spiritual study. Like Metapsychiatry, it is one of the many metaphysical spiritual pathways. It is particularly known for its emphasis on spiritual healing. When we understand our oneness with God, we are able to heal spiritually because we know that in divine Reality there is no human concept of anything or anybody to fix up. The more clearly we realise this, the more the human scene becomes subservient and harmonious. It falls into line with the overriding power and completeness of the infinite All.

Synonyms

Mind, Spirit, Soul, Principle, Life, Truth, and Love are the essence of Divinity and are frequently used synonyms for God in metaphysics. Being conscious of any of these qualities means being conscious of gratitude, happiness, completeness, and freedom. These spiritual elements are not only the structure of God but, wonderfully, they are also the structure of us. We are constituted of Divinity itself – nothing else, nothing less.

Mind is clear, intelligent, astounding in all its perfect detail, and beyond human manipulation. It cannot be held back by environment, education levels, inheritance or disposition.

Spirit changes everything. It changes what we want and what we love. Fear loses its hold on us. We are no longer attracted by the futile offerings of the world. We want and love spiritual happiness because we know that is the only thing that works.

Soul is that which impels us on our spiritual search. It is the voice within which tells us which way to go and lights the fire of hope, inspiration, passion, and enthusiasm.

Principle is that which is always solid, right, and enduring. It does not seek to control, hurt, stifle, judge or condemn. Principle wants only the best and highest good and insists on nothing less. It is not self-interested, tyrannical, demanding, petty or self-righteous. It is not tedious or judgmental. It is illuminating. It is the nurturing guide. It invokes trust and gratitude.

Life makes spiritual healing possible. Life is not material. It is not birth and death with all the in-between problems of susceptibility, pain, frailty, and fear. Life is spiritual.

Truth heals problems, conflict, and sickness because that which is not true can find no place to live within its energetic field. We do not have to make ourselves know the Truth. We let Truth shine.

Love is the foundation of existence. It is available and demonstrable to all equally. To know God is to know Love. A spiritual being loves because no other way than Love is known. It is not dependent on the presence of another. Nor is it halted by the actions of another.

Quotes

Angels are not etherealized human beings, evolving animal qualities in their wings; but they are celestial visitants, flying on spiritual, not material, pinions. Angels are pure thoughts from God, winged with Truth and Love. By giving earnest heed to these spiritual guides they tarry with us, and we entertain 'angels unawares. Mary Baker Eddy

The chief stones in the temple of Christian Science are to be found in the following postulates: that Life is God, good, and not evil; that Soul is sinless, not to be found in the body; that Spirit is not, and cannot be, materialized; that Life is not subject to death; that the spiritual real man has no birth, no material life, and no death. Mary Baker Eddy

Healing physical sickness is the smallest part of Christian Science. It is only the bugle call to thought and action, in the higher range of infinite goodness. Mary Baker Eddy

Where there is light, even the most long-standing darkness fades out. Light includes no darkness, and the consciousness of Truth contains no sense of error Truth heals because it knows nothing to heal. John Hargreaves

There is no place for a sick, sinning, sad or depleted sense of being in the divine and, as Truth supplants error, the divine and perfect sense of being is apparent everywhere. It was never absent. John Hargreaves

Mind-healing is never Truth applied to person or matter, but is the actual presence of Immanuel, God with us, precluding all unlike itself. It demands the practical living of our divinity – our identity with Truth – whereby that Mind is in us which was also in Christ Jesus, for in this Mind there is no place for anything needing to be healed. John Hargreaves

There is no life, truth, intelligence, nor substance in matter. All is infinite Mind and its infinite manifestation, for God is All-in-all. Spirit is immortal Truth; matter is mortal error. Spirit is the real and eternal; matter is the unreal and temporal. Spirit is God, and man is His image and likeness. Therefore man is not material; he is spiritual. Mary Baker Eddy

Man is not material; he is spiritual. Mary Baker Eddy

Become conscious for a single moment that Life and intelligence are purely spiritual, – neither in nor of matter, – and the body will then utter no complaints. If suffering from a belief in sickness, you will find yourself suddenly well. Mary Baker Eddy

God is Love. Can we ask Him to be more? God is intelligence. Can we inform the infinite Mind of anything He does not already comprehend? Mary Baker Eddy

The depth, breadth, height, might, majesty, and glory of infinite Love, fill all space. That is enough! Mary Baker Eddy

God is Love. More than this we cannot ask, higher we cannot look, further we cannot go. Mary Baker Eddy

God is universal; confined to no spot, defined by no dogma, appropriated by no sect. Not more to one than to all, is God demonstrable as divine Life, Truth, and Love: and His people are they that reflect Him – that reflect Love. Mary Baker Eddy

It is to know nothing but the loveliness, beauty, harmony, peace and joy of the divine Mind; it is never to lose sight of the loveliness of our own innate being. John Hargreaves

Love for God and man is the true incentive in both healing and teaching. Love inspires, illumes, designates and leads the way. Mary Baker Eddy

Spiritual Healing

Spiritual healing has always been a grand arena for the demonstration of metaphysics. When we see things spiritually there is nothing left to heal, nothing left to change, nothing left to restore or mend. All is beautifully perfect and infinite. The human healing that inevitably occurs, one way or another, is the shadow aligning itself correctly with divine Reality. It is the mist lifting with the morning rays of sun's warmth and light. It is the fog becoming less dense with Truth's brilliant clarity. When we understand the loveliness inherent in spiritual existence, our human existence reflects this loveliness. A consciousness which is imbued with divine Love sends healing to everything within its gaze and within its radius.

Fear

At the base of illness is fear. The removal of fear tends to have a healing effect on everything. How do we remove the fear? Even though this point is the most essential component of spiritual healing, it is also the most difficult to grasp. To human sense, our illnesses and problems seem very real. It takes dedicated spiritual study and practice to see that this is, in fact, not the case. When there is no fear, there is peace.

At a spiritual level, what we think has happened to us hasn't even occurred. From the higher perspective, it has not. This is how spiritual healers and metaphysicians heal. There is a recognition that God is all. Such are not words learned and repeated from a book. Knowing that God is all comes from the most inner of knowing, the highest of truths, the most demanding of pathways, the most egoless of disciplines. God is all means there is not ego. That, in essence, is enlightenment. In proportion that the human ego is operating, the realisation of Divinity is demonstrated or not. Healing of body, mind, and situation is the accompaniment. The allness of Divinity precludes anything unlike itself.

No Personal Healer

We do not try to become better personal healers. The goal is not to have a better human mind but to have less of a human mind. We are seeking to leave behind the personal sense of mind and become more fully conscious of the transpersonal Mind. Spiritual truth heals because when we are coming from a place of truth we can see that the thing which needs healing has no real substance to it. We do not look at a sick person and see a well person and then the sick person obliges by getting well. We look at someone and see a soul at home with God. If the individual has any receptivity to this idea, they too will start to see themselves in a different way. This transforms the human condition because it has to fall into line with a truth far greater than the flimsy pretensions of normal human existence. If we believe that we have the personal ability and power to heal then we are working from the premise of benevolent hypnotism. Such hypnotism is the exercise of one human mind over another human mind. We do not heal. God heals. Or, really, God just is. This reality leaves no room for anything to need healing.

The Process of Change

Chemicalization of thought is a metaphysical term referring to the mental and physical disturbance that frequently accompanies the process of change. It happens when loaded thoughts, emotions, and past events start to surface from the basement of our consciousness. Although not particularly enjoyable and often downright distressing, this process is immensely helpful in bringing to our awareness those thoughts that need healing and elevating.

Normally, when left to our own devices, most of us would prefer to live in ignorance if it didn't create so many problems. Chemicalization of thought is a way of getting our attention. It disturbs our equilibrium and the resulting heat eventually sorts the good from the bad stuff. An unsettled transitional stage is usually both inevitable and desirable. It is inevitable because of the nature of the human psyche. It is desirable because it ultimately leads to the separating of what is true and good from that which is false and destructive.

So, when we are suffering from the consequences of thoughts which are becoming painfully obvious to us, there is no need to despair. Don't feel bad about feeling bad. Don't be frightened of feeling afraid. Don't be angry about getting angry. There is no need to give up when we are feeling depressed. Nor should we be dismayed at the grief which often accompanies the outgrowing of anything which needs outgrowing. We can be glad that our soul is speaking to us and pushing us onwards. We frequently need to persevere with a period of inner turmoil before the dust can settle and be swept out the door.

Discerning Thoughts

All effective spiritual healers intuitively sense, to some extent, which human thoughts are causing a particular illness or blocking a healing. Many healers find that it is at the point of waking up to an unrecognised thought that real progress is made with a client. It is at that moment of, "Ah, that's what I've been thinking. Why did I not see it before?" Often, it is a fear, an unforgiven hurt, a silent resentment left to grow, a jealousy, a sense of revenge, guilt for a regretted action or a false responsibility. Understanding our thinking becomes supremely important to us when we know that our thoughts wield such an influence over our peace of mind and health. As we continue on the path, we will find that thoughts we could easily tolerate within a less developed consciousness become increasingly intolerable and offensive to a more developed consciousness.

A Knowledge of Error

It is important to healing that we have a knowledge of error. We, generally, need to understand the nature of the misguided thought or error so that we can knowingly replace it with something much better and more conducive to health. A healer needs to be sensitive about the right moment to reveal these erroneous thoughts. The timing of this revelation is often crucial to the person being able to see the mistake. One must be tuned into divine wisdom and guidance.

Although understanding thought is often pivotal in a healing, we do not build up the harmful thought to even greater proportions. Unhealthy thoughts are revealed in order to be dismissed. When an error is exposed to the light, it is uncovered as nothing and not as something which has then got to be dealt with. The error is not only nothing to do with us; it does not exist. It is because of the allness of Truth that anything else has to be nothing. God is not in the illness, the argument, the lack, the disappointment, the grief or the fear. We must not work against ourselves by identifying with the problem and the person having the problem and then ask God to fix it up. We look away from the whole picture of a mortal, sick or well, to the spiritual idea which is infinite, all-existent, and eternal. We see the perfection of creation. Spiritually speaking, health is an awareness of divine perfection.

Monitoring the content of our thoughts is of paramount importance. Every thought of imperfection which is allowed to take root and grow will cause us harm. Of course, in the face of illness, everyone must follow whatever means of healing they feel is right for them in the situation – whether it be medical, alternative, spiritual or a combination. Nevertheless, it is a great protection to understand the power of thought and to refuse entry to any thought that one does not want realised in the body. Entry to the body is by passageway of the mind.

Mind Reading and Psychic Ability

Mind reading and psychic ability which have come from a genuine spiritual interest are for the purpose of good. They are not used in an intrusive, destructive, or condemnatory way. The intention is to help and heal. Extra sensory abilities tend to grow naturally for the spiritual student, along with an insightful understanding of human nature. They can occur in a variety of ways from the simple to the substantial such as:

1. Knowing who is on the phone before answering. (This article was written before the time of our mobiles telling us who is on the phone!)
2. Unexpectedly thinking or dreaming of someone and then having that person contact us.
3. Knowing what someone is going to say or do.
4. Knowing what someone really means when they say something even if it is the opposite of what they have just said in words.
5. Having an insistent feeling when something is not right. Some years ago, I went on a five-day spiritual retreat to Alice Springs in the desert country of central Australia. At dawn, on the first morning, I climbed up the Macdonnell Ranges on my own. They were within metres of the place I stayed. They are not very high, only several hundred metres. They are red, rocky, old, and grand. It was very quiet and still. The

63

rock wallabies were keeping an eye on me from a distance. I climbed right to the top and could then see down the other side of the range into the town of Alice Springs. The sun on the great expanse of ranges and desert land was intensely light and beautiful. As always in that part of the world, there was a vast, glowing sky. Everywhere I looked was immense and glorious. It was beauty and spiritual power in its most raw form.

During that first day, the group had several meditations. In the meditations, I had a strange experience of feeling like I was falling down a cliff. Later that day, I told the retreat leader about it. She asked me what sort of cliffs they were. I told her that they were red and rocky like the ones I had seen that morning. She explained that a few days ago someone had fallen down one of the cliffs in the very area where I was walking. The person was still in hospital in a serious condition. I then knew that it was a request for prayer from the person who was recovering. I also felt it was a request from the mountain, as nature does not like to carry the memory of an accident. I worked on it for a day and then the feeling left me and I was not troubled about the situation anymore.

6. Listening to messages and warnings not originating from our own thought. One day, when I was seven months pregnant with my youngest child and walking my German shepherd, I became frightened by the aggressive behaviour of another dog who seemed to be escaping from his property. To avoid the dog, I was going to cross a busy road without looking properly. Just before stepping onto the road, an inner voice said commandingly, *Stop!* I stopped. Two

seconds later, a car zoomed past, inches away from me. I was shocked. My intention was to cross the road. An intuitive message had saved us all. I walked home to my young family in awe.

7. Knowing whether to trust someone or not, even though you may have only just met the person. Many years ago on arriving in a new community, I was instantly struck by a sense of friendship upon being introduced to a woman there. I was drawn to her warmth but, more than that, I felt I knew her well. I wanted to say something like, *Oh, how lovely. Now we are both here.* Of course, one cannot say that to a stranger so I settled with a barely contained, "Oh, you are nice!" which was not really appropriate either.

8. Passing people on the street and sensing their energy, either good or not so good.

9. Receiving ideas and instructions in our sleep and having visits from people while we are asleep. The visitors may be living individuals, passed on souls, or spiritual beings. They may give advice or suggestions. Sometimes, simply the memory of their presence will spark an idea or give an answer to a question that was being pondered. They may bring love and reassurance.

10. Sensing someone's jealousy. We are a great deal safer once we have learned to listen to our inner voice about who is jealous of us and who wishes us harm. When this is understood, we are able to protect ourselves more effectively, and we can work on forgiving the other person who is acting out the normal human drama. Many people endure relentless jealousy from relatives, friends, colleagues, and acquaintances. They are not able to adequately protect themselves because they feel that their instinct must be wrong and that the person couldn't be thinking that way about them. Jealousy always seeks to harm in

proportion to its intensity. It makes no difference if the person is conscious or not of their jealous intent. It is our responsibility to protect ourselves and our loved ones. Ignorance and naivety are dangerous.

11. Sensing the presence of an animal spirit. Our family has always had dogs, in fact, a pack of dogs. Several years had passed since my first German shepherd had died and, at that stage, I wasn't planning on getting another. However, I started to have a recurring dream about a German shepherd that I didn't know. Soon after, when my preschool son and I were out, he pointed to a sign that I hadn't seen and he told me that German shepherd pups were for sale. There was no picture on the sign and my son couldn't read but, somehow, he not only knew what the sign said but he also knew it was important to tell me. I hadn't mentioned anything about another dog to him. As it turned out, one of those pups became ours.

A year or so after the pup arrived, it was time for one of our old dogs to move on. He was a wonderful, faithful little dog who had been a best friend to my oldest son during his childhood and had since taken on guard duties with my much younger son. I came downstairs early in the morning and went to let the dogs out, as usual. The old dog was lying on the floor unconscious and I could see that he had been there for a while. As soon as I saw him, I knew it was time for him to go. I stroked him and told him, "Don't be afraid to go, old friend. You've done a wonderful job. Thank-you so much for all you have done for us, for loving us, and being a beautiful friend." His breathing changed and he seemed to relax. I went to get dressed so that I could take him to the vet but when I came back downstairs, he was gone. He had waited to say, *Good-bye, I love you all but I have to go now.* He seemed to be also waiting for me to reassure him that there was nothing to be afraid of.

These experiences could come from psychic awareness, an acute understanding of human nature, or Divine inspiration. Extrasensory abilities are naturally developed within us by being more receptive to the subtle and finer messages constantly around us. We all have extrasensory, as well as sensory faculties. We can all learn to intelligently assess human nature. We all are spiritual beings, at home in the domain of inspired thought.

Reading the One Mind

While many spiritually minded individuals have discovered they have some amount of psychic ability, there are also psychic people who have no interest in connecting with the Divine. As helpful as it can be, psychic ability is no indicator of spiritual maturity. In the higher realm of Spirit there is the reading of the one Mind rather than the reading of the many minds. From the standpoint of Spirit there is no personal mind or ego to read. Understanding this is a protection from any would-be destructive or negative psychic energy. That which finds no footing in divine Reality is powerless to exert its presence or influence and is not to be feared.

I Am Not Here

If we become aware that someone is sending thoughts of ill will in our direction, we do not argue with the apparent reality of malice. To do so would give it more substance. We remove the personal sense of the other person and of ourself. This negates the fear and the power of ill will. When there is no person, there is no room for the sad and weak pretence of personal power. When the concept of power apart from God has been recognised for the nothingness that it truly is then it will be eliminated. In its place will flood in the safety, peace, purity, and uncontaminated radiance of Love.

Guarding Our Thoughts

The media is a great communicator of harmful thought. Fear, anger, ugliness, violence, condemnation, and the promotion of damaging values are widespread in the media's presentation. Watch and read with an awareness that what is being conveyed is not what you want to be unreservedly taking in. It is a dream or, generally, a nightmare that has its audience within its grasp. It is neither where we belong nor where we wish to linger. Watch and listen with compassion and love but from a distance. Instead of contributing to the general negative hysteria, we are calming, healing, and erasing it. We know that we are infinitely loved and cared for and that every other soul is also loved. We need to guard ourselves against any idea, person or phenomenon which threatens this sense. This precious knowledge is worth protecting. Remain awake.

Conversations and Gossip

One of the first serious spiritual practices I learned in my early twenties was to watch what I was talking about. It is unfortunate but not surprising that most people have no idea what they are saying, to whom, and the consequences of that on themselves and others. If we want to be happy; don't gossip, don't spread hate, don't talk about other people, don't spread fear, don't complain, don't relay stories which are detrimental to the well-being of those around us. That will cut out the vast majority of most people's conversations. There is a time for honest, well-intentioned directness but it is not found in common conversation and it is a learned skill. Be a bringer of peace and healing. It's a discipline, for sure, but one that will transform our lives.

As spiritual students, we need to be careful that the influence we have on other people in our conversations is for good only. We also need to be careful about what we allow into our own thoughts. We become conscious of what we do and say, and of what we see and hear. We do not engage in idle or intentional gossip which undermines someone else's integrity or which spreads the seeds of fear by talking unthinkingly about illness, disasters, and all the other fears that run rampant in the world. We may talk lightly but never carelessly and we constantly keep at bay the flow of common, ignorant thought which runs its damaging course through the pathways of ordinary human conversation. Whenever there is an opportunity, our conversation seeks to validate, in some humble way, the beauty and love which constantly upholds us all.

It is helpful to remember that true love is communicated nonverbally. It is set by our intention. If our intention is not at a level that is gracious, compassionate, and loving then no amount of sweet talk will ever convince the recipient of our goodwill. On the other hand, if our inner-being radiates peace and unselfish care then our presence will have a reassuring, uplifting, and healing effect, no matter what we say or omit to say. The recipient of our words will have a tendency to respect and appreciate us and will gravitate towards us.

Quotes

Healing is the absolute acknowledgment of the ever-presence of infinite perfection. Mary Baker Eddy

Healing is the discovery that there was nothing wrong to begin with. Thomas Hora

There is no place for a sick, sinning, sad or depleted sense of being in the divine and, as Truth supplants error, the divine and perfect sense of being is apparent everywhere. It was never absent. John Hargreaves

All that really exists is the divine Mind and its idea, and in this Mind the entire being is found harmonious and eternal. Mary Baker Eddy

When the illusion of sickness or sin tempts you, cling steadfastly to God and his idea. Allow nothing but his likeness to abide in your thought. Let neither fear nor doubt overshadow your dear sense and calm trust, that life harmonious can destroy any painful sense of that which Life is not. Mary Baker Eddy

Always begin your treatment by allaying the fear of patients. Watch the result of this simple rule and you will find that it alleviates the symptoms of every disease. If you succeed in wholly removing the fear, your patient is healed. Mary Baker Eddy

Truth is real, and error is unreal. Mary Baker Eddy

The [metaphysician] will be calm in the presence of both sin and disease, knowing as he does, that Life is God and God is All. Mary Baker Eddy

Nothing real can be threatened.
Nothing unreal exists.
Herein lies the peace of God. A Course in Miracles

When we fully understand our relation to the Divine, we can have no other Mind but His – no other Love, wisdom, or Truth, no other sense of Life, and no consciousness of the existence of matter or error. Mary Baker Eddy

Nothing is ever going on but Mind unfolding its own spiritual idea. Nothing can resist, obstruct, or delay that which is already omnipresent and omnipotent. That which emerges into light is the completeness of being that is already here. This Mind is your Mind and your Life, knowing only the perfection of its own being. It knows nothing to heal – and that is why it heals. John Hargreaves

The sun shines. It is not in the business of eliminating darkness. It is in the business of being light, and entirely incidental to this the darkness flees in its presence. John Hargreaves

When one is healed nothing has really happened to him; there is just less of the mist of mortal mind and more reality revealed in consciousness. Bicknell Young

Chemicalization is the upheaval produced when immortal Truth is destroying erroneous mortal belief.

Mental chemicalization brings sin and sickness to the surface, forming impurities to pass away, as is the case with the fermenting liquid. Mary Baker Eddy

Awakening from a false sense, from the illusion of life in matter, is a blessing, not an affliction, however painful it may claim to be. It is always a blessing to be undeceived. Bicknell Young

Do not murmur or grieve or feel self-pity or discouragement over the need for uncovering and destroying deeper errors. Rather rejoice that the good work goes on, and that it is because Truth and Love are unfolding in and as your consciousness that these aggressive mental suggestions are being uncovered – not only in your own consciousness, but in the universal consciousness as well. Bicknell Young

Whoever reaches this point of moral culture and goodness cannot injure others, but must do them good. The greater or lesser ability of a [metaphysician] to discern thought scientifically depends upon his genuine spirituality. It is important to success in healing, and is one of the special characteristics thereof. Mary Baker Eddy

By not perceiving vital metaphysical points, not seeing how mortal mind affects the body – acting beneficially or injuriously on the health, as well as on the morals and the happiness of mortals – we are misled in our conclusions and methods. Mary Baker Eddy

Mesmeric beliefs that have been latent in your thinking, unknown, become aggressive and more apparent to you as Truth and Love unfold in your thinking. Truth brings them to the surface, and uncovers them to you until their nothingness in the light of unfolding Truth and Love, appears. Bicknell Young

When false human beliefs learn even a little of their own falsity, they begin to disappear. A knowledge of error and of its operations must precede that understanding of Truth which destroys error. Mary Baker Eddy

All that you are called upon to do is to get rid of the beliefs in your own consciousness, and trust the unfolding idea to get rid of the beliefs in everyone's consciousness. Bicknell Young

Let the unfolding idea, the progressing, unfolding idea, bring these uncoverings to the individual. Let Truth uncover error through progressive unfoldment. Bicknell Young

It is most important to recognize that when an error appears, it is appearing to disappear. Bicknell Young

Our Master easily read the thoughts of mankind, and this insight better enabled him to direct those thoughts aright. Our Master read mortal mind on a scientific basis, that of the omnipresence of Mind. An approximation of this discernment indicates spiritual growth and union with the infinite capacities of the one Mind. Jesus could injure no one by his Mind-reading. The effect of his Mind was always to heal and to save, and this is the only genuine Science of reading mortal mind. Mary Baker Eddy

Such intuitions reveal whatever constitutes and perpetuates harmony, enabling one to do good, but not evil. You will reach the perfect Science of healing when you are able to read the human mind after this manner and discern the error you would destroy. Mary Baker Eddy

When sufficiently advanced in [metaphysical] Science to be in harmony with the truth of being, men become seers and prophets involuntarily. Acquaintance with the Science of being enables us to commune more largely with the divine Mind, to foresee and foretell events which concern the universal welfare, to be divinely inspired – yea, to reach the range of fetterless Mind. Mary Baker Eddy

When we fully understand our relation to the Divine, we can have no other Mind but His – no other Love, wisdom, or Truth, no other sense of Life. Mary Baker Eddy

Nothing is real and eternal, – nothing is Spirit, – but God and His idea. Mary Baker Eddy

The calm, strong currents of true spirituality, the manifestations of which are health, purity and self-immolation, must deepen human experience, until the beliefs of mortal existence are seen to be a bald imposition, and sin, disease, and death give everlasting place to the scientific demonstration of divine Spirit and to God's spiritual, perfect man. Mary Baker Eddy

Stand porter at the door of thought. Admitting only such conclusions as you wish realized in bodily results, you will control yourself harmoniously. Mary Baker Eddy

Health is the consciousness of the unreality of pain and disease; or, rather, the absolute consciousness of harmony and of nothing else. Mary Baker Eddy

A physical diagnosis of disease – since mortal mind must be the cause of disease – tends to induce disease. Mary Baker Eddy

It is well to be calm in sickness;, to be hopeful is still better; but to understand that sickness is not real and that Truth can destroy its seeming reality, is best of all, for this understanding is the universal and perfect remedy. Mary Baker Eddy

The press unwittingly sends forth many sorrows and diseases among the human family. It does this by giving names to diseases and by printing long descriptions which mirror images of disease distinctly in thought. Mary Baker Eddy

If thought yields its dominion to other powers, it cannot outline on the body its own beautiful images, but it effaces them and delineates foreign agents, called sin and disease. Mary Baker Eddy

The Human Experience

Spiritual awareness transfers into our human experience as loving and satisfying relationships, rewarding and remunerative work, trouble free health, and so on. Good manifests in our human life in creative and unbounded forms. All levels of being harmonise and flow into the expression of goodness and grace.

Material Supply

Like all aspects of the human condition, money is a reflection of a nonmaterial universe. Supply, in any form, is demonstrated according to the law of attraction and our destiny. As energetic beings living in a harmonious and energetic world, it is available and right for the circumstance.

Some years ago, my usual means of paying my children's private school fees became suddenly unavailable, and it was to remain so indefinitely. A few days before finding out about the aborted income for the school fees, I discovered that I was to receive a totally unexpected inheritance. It came from an uncle who I rarely saw. He was a pensioner and so it was very surprising that he had any money to give to anyone. The inheritance was exactly what was needed to cover two years of school fees for two dependents – a considerable amount. When the two years had elapsed and the inheritance had been used, alternative means for paying the school fees became spontaneously available. Whatever we need can come from wherever it is now.

Translating Things into Thoughts

In order to elevate our human experience, we translate the material into its spiritual essence. Home is love, peace, and nurturing. Family is spiritual co-habitation, respect, and appreciation for another's existence. Work is purpose, service, creativity, and usefulness. Money is freedom and generosity. Success is goodwill, energy, intelligence, and initiative. In this way, we will find that supply, in its deepest sense, is ever available. We will also find that it will not have the tendency to turn sour.

Companionship and Love

Companionship, love, and support are everywhere and ever-present. They are the natural outflow of divinity. The greater our sense of primary divine connection, the more easily will these beautiful resources of Life be attracted into our existence. How could it be otherwise since we are reflecting not our own but Life's wonderful, appealing, and valuable qualities?

We do not have the right to dictate to God in which manner this love will be revealed in our life. We are completely open to all the varied and, sometimes, unexpected ways in which Love will choose to bless us and use us. That is all we will ever need to ensure our happiness. One who knows their connection with divine Love can never feel the isolation of loneliness or the fear of being rejected or deserted. One cannot be apart from or turned away from a Love which knows no parting and is present and available under all circumstances.

No Love is Lovely but the Divine

Much misery in caused in relationships by the expectation that the other person can and should be a personal provider of good for us. This expectation brings an endless array of problems and is one which we need to outgrow as individuals who are seeking freedom from the troubles of the human condition. No person is able to give what only divine Love can give. Relationships, of their own power, cannot give us the love and happiness that really have a Divine, not human, origin. We don't ask from other people what only God can supply.

All desirable qualities are, in essence, spiritual ideas. Beauty, purity, love, kindness, warmth, joy, humour, creativity, talent, power, intelligence, protection, and forthrightness are expressions of God manifest in the world. We appreciate every lovely quality that comes to us through the life of another but, ultimately, God is the source of all good, not another person. Our connection with others is primarily based on letting the inner spiritual beauty spring forth into life in the many and varied ways it will choose to do so. Our happiness, peace, safety, and individual development is protected and we find that all things will work together for good.

Sexual Expression

Many good people carry with them sexual inhibitions and guilt. Sexual desires are a normal and natural part of being human. Avoidance, fear, guilt, and prudishness about sex have no place in a healthy, balanced perspective on life. Like many people, I grew up with numerous prohibitive and unhealthy concepts about my body and sexuality in general. As a raised Catholic, it almost goes without saying. These concepts were brought to the surface and dispelled much later when I took up ice skating. Like dancing, the world of ice skating is based on a natural feeling that bodies are genuinely beautiful. The body is not a vessel for unwanted or shameful tendencies. It is, in fact, the very instrument which channels the beauty, skill, and wonder of the sport/art form. These ideas helped me to release the outgrown, repressive concepts which I had previously held both consciously and unconsciously.

If we are relaxed, grateful, considerate, and confident then our sexual relationship with our loved one will probably be happy, problem-free, and satisfying for both people or, at least, it will be moving in that direction. We can acquire an attitude to sex which is liberating, caring, and open. From a spiritual perspective, we can enjoy it in the same way that we enjoy every other beautiful and pleasant thing in the human experience – with not too much attachment but not repressive and condemnatory.

The Longing for Oneness

Sex, like everything else, is good or bad, helpful or unhelpful, pleasant or painful, fulfilling or demoralizing based on the thoughts of the participants. Within the context of love, sex is a force for good. For many people, a loving sexual connection is actually the closest they ever get to a transcendent sense of benevolence, bliss, and that feeling of *all is well* – the closest they get to God. This is because loving, sexual oneness is the shadow of true, spiritual Oneness. As such, it carries with it some of the same elements, some of the same promise. The desire for physical unity is really representative of the deeper desire for spiritual completeness. Within a spontaneous, playful, respectful, and unselfish context sexual closeness is a channel for light but it cannot fulfil our deepest yearnings.

Moving Meditation

As spiritual students, if we wish to, we can use our sexual life with our partner as a *moving meditation*. Yoga is often referred to as a moving meditation. In yoga, one goes deeply inward, connecting with the Divine while at the same time moving the body in a way that has a beneficial and life-enhancing effect. One does not force the pose or fall asleep. It is awake, reverent attention. Similarly, walking can become an opportunity to move the body easily, graciously, and freely while drawing within to the non-dimensional ease, grace, and freedom which supports the inner Universe. Dancing with a partner becomes a consensual sharing of energy where the two individuals can, ideally, take their cue from the great flowing Movement beyond themselves. Likewise, sex can also become a consensual sharing of body, mind, and spirit. It can be an opportunity to expand the physicality of the experience into the very beat of Life which is always alive, responsive, and fulfilling and has a positive effect on those involved.

Creativity and Beauty

In creative pursuits, we connect with the qualities of our inner being. We open up to the invisible, yet, powerful world of Spirit. It carries with it all the immensity, love, power, wisdom, beauty, and harmony of the Universe. We are part of it. We allow it to flow through us with the beautiful feeling and potency of that which supports the entire world and more. We are a channel for universal energy, passion, and soul. It is energy which explodes into all creative activity. It is passion which gives us courage and unlimited vision. It is soul which moves us beyond our own limited world to see the interconnectedness of all humanity.

This spiritual world is always available to us. We don't need to make it happen. It is already here. We just need to see it, be part of it, open to it. Even a slight move in that direction is enough for Love to come rushing in. Under the influence of the divine Presence all of our activities became more beautiful, expressive, healing, and uplifting.

Grief

Grieving is commonly experienced in the wake of all sorts of apparent losses, not just death. Every time we feel we have lost something of value, we tend to grieve. We deny it. We bargain to try to make the loss less painful. We get angry. We get depressed. We, sometimes, get sick. And if all goes well, we eventually accept it. This is the human process. The spiritual process, however, takes on a different dimension. On losing a friend, I asked healer and author, John Hargreaves, who was my spiritual teacher at that time, to help me get over the grief and sadness. Grief, after all, can be a very painful experience. It is a pain which no medicine can relieve. It comes from a place so deep in our heart that we feel nothing can reach it.

It was pointed out to me that the Infinite One cannot be torn apart from itself. It is our personification of good, our belief that it belongs to a personal identity which makes grief possible. And it is our understanding of universal good, of God's being everywhere and in everything which heals it. The qualities and abilities which we may miss in someone are not missing from Life. Every beautiful and wonderful quality in someone is abundantly present and waiting to be recognised in all of life's great symphony.

John said, "Our understanding of our relationship to God makes human relationships subservient to Principle. As the emanation of God we come forth permanently complete.

Completeness is not a personal state to lose or regain but results from the fact that we live as the experience of Love itself. How this works out in our life is up to God. We stay in our exalted position which is at peace and from which the unfolding of ideas goes on. We cannot miss out on anything. The Law of Intelligence does not condemn or punish. It is entirely benevolent."

Moral Freedom

At a certain level of consciousness, we need and benefit from the restraints of moral and ethical boundaries. However, those who have attained a spiritual degree of consciousness have a declining need for these boundaries because they no longer want anything except what is loving, for the highest good, and in everyone's best interest. The spiritual person has a deep and innately good view of all. They do not have to rely on moral boundaries to protect themselves and others. They do not need artificial constraints to maintain their spiritual progress and clarity. They know that they will be continually guided to respond to life's issues in ways that can only be good. They have freedom to respond to spiritual ideas, knowing that their motives, thoughts, words, and actions are for the benefit of all and can hurt no one. Their reliance is on Spirit. This is freedom.

Conscience is a legitimate check on thought that may wander into harmful territory. However, when we are in alignment with God, the necessity for our conscience to maintain its unrelenting, guarding position is released. Choices are more frequently made on the basis of spiritual intuition which is a direct link to divine Good. Spiritual intuition encompasses knowledge we may not yet be consciously aware of, for instance, there may be many extenuating circumstances in a situation which we may not know but the divine Mind does.

Quotes

Divine Love always has met and always will meet every human need. The miracle of grace is no miracle to Love. Mary Baker Eddy

Hold thought steadfastly to the enduring, the good, and the true, and you will bring these into your experience proportionally to their occupancy of your thoughts. Mary Baker Eddy

I do not lack anything.
I do not lack wisdom or love.
I do not lack judgment or intelligence.
I do not lack energy or industry.
I do not lack and cannot lack anything or the means by which to acquire anything.
I am not outside infinity. Mary Baker Eddy

Our Father is rich and will not deprive us of one good thing, but will add continually to our storehouse of blessings. Everything belongs to God. It is ours now as His reflection for there are no debts in divine Love. Mary Baker Eddy

Supply is omnipresent and unlimited, and is always where you are and what you need. It is liable to show itself to you through millions of channels. Therefore open up all the channels and let it come in. Keep yourself in a state of non-surprise. Gain a mental attitude in which nothing in the way of supply will surprise you. You are not the victim of any circumstance; you are the child of God. Mary Baker Eddy

Metaphysics resolves things into thoughts, and exchanges the objects of sense for the ideas of Soul. Mary Baker Eddy

A table, an automobile, a house, and all things which appear to meet the needs of humanity today, are really only a material, limited sense of what is actually present as ideas of completeness, wholeness, satisfaction, ease – that which contributes to a perfect state of being. When understood as Love manifested as ideas and not as the material things they appear to be, they will always bless us, always add to our comfort, happiness and wellbeing, and always satisfy us. There never will be too much or too little – either of which is hampering and limiting. Bicknell Young

Tones of the human mind may be different, but they should be concordant in order to blend properly. Unselfish ambition, noble life-motives, and purity – these constituents of thought, mingling, constitute individually and collectively true happiness, strength, and permanence. Mary Baker Eddy

The form, the activity of Love, we cannot outline. Bicknell Young

Soul has infinite resources with which to bless mankind, and happiness would be more readily attained and would be more secure in our keeping, if sought in Soul. Mary Baker Eddy

No wisdom is wise but His wisdom; no truth is true, no love is lovely, no life is Life but the divine; no good is, but the good God bestows. Mary Baker Eddy

When we realize that Life is Spirit, never in nor of matter, this understanding will expand into self-completeness, finding all in God, good, and needing no other consciousness. Mary Baker Eddy

Oftentimes in denying yourself pleasure you do but store the desire in the recesses of your being.
Who knows but that which seems omitted today, waits for tomorrow? Kahlil Gibran

Ay, in very truth, pleasure is a freedom-song.
And I fain would have you sing it with fullness of heart; yet I would not have you lose your hearts in the singing. Kahlil Gibran

The recipe for beauty is to have less illusion and more Soul, to retreat from the belief of pain or pleasure in the body into the unchanging calm and glorious freedom of spiritual harmony. Mary Baker Eddy

Whatever holds human thought in line with unselfed love, receives directly the divine power. Mary Baker Eddy

God fashions all things, after His own likeness. Life is reflected in existence, Truth in truthfulness, God in goodness, which impart their own peace and permanence. Love, redolent with unselfishness, bathes all in beauty and light. The grass beneath our feet silently exclaims, 'The meek shall inherit the earth.' The modest arbutus sends her sweet breath to heaven. The great rock gives shadow and shelter. The sunlight glints from the church-dome, glances into the prison-cell, glides into the sick-chamber, brightens the flower, beautifies the landscape, blesses the earth.

Man, made in His likeness, possesses and reflects God's dominion over all the earth. Mary Baker Eddy

Comeliness and grace are independent of matter. Being possesses its qualities before they are perceived humanly. Beauty is a thing of life, which dwells forever in the eternal Mind and reflects the charms of His goodness in expression, form, outline and colour. It is Love which paints the petal with myriad hues, glances in the warm sunbeam, arches the cloud with the bow of beauty, blazons the night with starry gems, and covers the earth with loveliness. Mary Baker Eddy

Divine Love is never so near as when all earthly joys seem most afar. Mary Baker Eddy

Who that has felt the loss of human peace has not gained stronger desires for spiritual joy? The loss of earthly hopes and pleasures brightens the ascending path of many a heart. The pains of sense quickly inform us that the pleasures of sense are mortal and that joy is spiritual. Mary Baker Eddy

As the emanation of God we come forth permanently complete. Completeness is not a personal state to lose or regain but results from the fact that we live as the experience of Love itself. How this works out in our life is up to God, but we stay in our exalted position which is at peace, and from which the unfolding of ideas goes on. We cannot miss out on anything. The Law of Intelligence does not condemn or punish. It is entirely benevolent. John Hargreaves

God, Spirit, dwelling in infinite light and harmony from which emanates the true idea, is never reflected by aught but the good. Mary Baker Eddy

There is moral freedom in Soul. Mary Baker Eddy

Each Successive Stage

One evening, I became aware of two important, dawning ideas. The first idea was that it was time to start my practice as a spiritual healer and counsellor. I wished to expand my spiritual influence. The second emerging idea was an unanticipated but definite sense that the purpose of my relationship had been met and that it would not be in either person's best long-term interest to remain life partners. Although my husband and I had been living from a different understanding of life, there had been a sense of purpose, love, and gratitude in the relationship and so it had felt right. We had been able to safely journey through several serious challenges. It seemed that those tasks had been completed. Further, it seemed clear that where we needed to go next would not accommodate us going together.

Neither Married nor Not Married

When I initially brought up the matter, John Hargreaves wisely advised me:

1. "You will not find right and wrong within the dream." This was a reminder to not look for answers in the human drama where they cannot be found.
2. "Marriage belongs to the time world and is therefore a concession but not the Truth. In the infinite One there is nothing else to marry. This does not mean that you abandon the human but, rather, that the human is found increasingly to be the Divine appearing in a language that is perceptible. The human, imbued with the Divine, begins to lose the human frailty of its basis." Marriage is a human arrangement. It may be a very good and positive arrangement but it is an aspect of the material world.

Within the divine consciousness there is no need for marriage because true marriage or Oneness is with the Divine. There can be no separation from the completeness which is our true and total being. Spiritual truth is a solitary matter.

3. "Take this step by step. Do not outline or feel that you have some great decision to make but know that God is not separate from the wisdom that the all-wise bestows and remember that at every level of experience, the only law is that of divine Love insisting on the highest good. This may mean being together happily or going different ways. There is nothing sacrosanct about either course."

The Dawn of Ideas

Everyone is a unique expression of God, with a unique life path. As such, life's decisions are a matter between each individual and God. They will be spiritually and humanly worked out, step by step. As with all of life's decisions, the essential requirements to move ahead in a beneficial way are honesty, love, unselfishness, a desire for good in everyone's life, lack of ill-will, disregard of what other people think of us, and courage. With these qualities on board, the best solution will be reached to everyone's eventual benefit.

In my last contact with John a short while before his passing, he said, "Remember that nothing has ever taken place as person. It is always that you are divinely shedding some aspect of the human mind, which you have outgrown. Keep it all impersonal. Nothing is ever present as person but always as God-being. Always begin with God, not man. There is no personal ego and never was."

Gratitude Prayer

May we be grateful for everything good.
Good is everything.
May we remember that God is the only Love.
May our eyes radiate nonconditional benevolence.
May our awareness be of spiritual perfection.
May our freedom be boundless.
May we know the loveliness of love.
May the Divine presence fill our consciousness.
May we feel the magnificent capacity of Life.
May our touch be uplifting.
May our influence be a blessing.
May we feel the immensity of Divinity.
May we know the sublime Love that we are part of.
May it sustain us.
It is us.

Quotes

Each successive stage of experience unfolds new views of divine goodness and love. Mary Baker Eddy

One must fulfil one's mission without timidity or dissimulation, for to be well done, the work must be done unselfishly. Mary Baker Eddy

Neglect not the gift that is in thee. The Bible

When you become aware of the nature of this gift, when you discover the channel through which your particular message is to be delivered to the world, lend all of your energies to make the gift perfect and to keep the channel free of obstructions. Through this gift and this message, salvation will come to you as well as to others. You can have all the power in all ways, that you need; and you will have as much as you desire and seek for, if you live – not after the flesh, but after the spirit, looking to "the things that are above." Aim for perfection. Perfection is God. Remember, too, that this work has been delegated to you to do, can be done by none other; therefore be faithful, be true. Trust. Nora Holm

Marriage should signify a union of hearts. Mary Baker Eddy

Furthermore, the time cometh of which Jesus spoke, when he declared that in the resurrection there should be no more marrying or giving in marriage, but man would be as the angels. Mary Baker Eddy

Man is neither married nor not married. Thomas Hora

God is man's only real relative on earth and in heaven. Mary Baker Eddy

You will not find right and wrong within the dream. John Hargreaves

Marriage belongs to the time world and is therefore a concession but not the Truth. In the infinite One there is nothing else to marry! This does not mean that you abandon the human but, rather, that the human is found increasingly to be the divine appearing in a language that is perceptible. The human, imbued with the divine, begins to lose the human frailty of its basis. John Hargreaves

Take this step by step. Do not outline or feel that you have some great decision to make, but know that God is not separate from the wisdom that the all-wise bestows and remember that at every level of experience, the only law is that of divine Love insisting on the highest good. This may mean being together happily or going different ways. There is nothing sacrosanct about either course. John Hargreaves

Through divine Science, Spirit, God, unites understanding to eternal harmony. The calm and exalted thought or spiritual apprehension is at peace. Thus the dawn of ideas goes on, forming each successive stage of progress. Mary Baker Eddy

When asked by a wife or a husband important questions concerning their happiness, the substance of my reply is: God will guide you. Mary Baker Eddy

Work out the greatest good to the greatest number, before you are sure of being a fit counsellor. Mary Baker Eddy

Wisdom in human action begins with what is nearest right under the circumstances. Mary Baker Eddy

To reckon the universal cost and gain, as well as thine own, is right in every state and stage of being. Mary Baker Eddy

[Spirituality] lifts humanity higher in the scale of harmony, and must ultimately break all bonds that hinder progress. Mary Baker Eddy

Spirit, God, gathers unformed thoughts into their proper channels, and unfolds these thoughts, even as He opens the petals of a holy purpose in order that the purpose may appear. Mary Baker Eddy

Goodness never fails to receive its reward, for goodness makes life a blessing. As an active portion of one stupendous whole, goodness identifies man with universal good. Mary Baker Eddy

I am able to impart truth, health, and happiness, and this is my reason for existing. Mary Baker Eddy

No truth can be stereotyped. Teachers, in any field, can help us on our way, but they cannot define or control the manifold paths of progress. The only proof of understanding is demonstration. John Hargreaves

Remember that nothing has ever taken place as person. It is always that you are divinely shedding some aspect of the human mind, which you have outgrown. Keep it all impersonal. Nothing is ever present as person but always as God-being. Always begin with God, not man. There is no personal ego and never was. John Hargreaves

About the Author

Donna shares her love for the Divine and mankind with a large international audience.

All links https://linktr.ee/donnagoddard

The author acknowledges the PAGL Foundation for permission to use passages from the works of Dr Thomas Hora, founder of Metapsychiatry. All rights reserved. Visit www.pagl.org

Also visit www.themetaway.com for Metapsychiatry.

The writings of Mary Baker Eddy can be found at www.christianscience.com

Also visit www.thebookmark.com for older Christian Science writings.

The author acknowledges Mulberry Press for permission to use passages from the works of John Hargreaves and from my own personal letters. The writings of John Hargreaves can be found at www.mulberrypress.com

Ratings and Reviews

If you have enjoyed this book, I would be most grateful for any ratings/reviews on Amazon or elsewhere. Thank you.

Printed in Great Britain
by Amazon